ILLINOIS PRAIRIE DISTRICT PUBLIC LIBRARY

Hq. Metamora, Illinois

RULES

1. Books may be kept for three weeks.
2. A fine of five cents a day will be charged on each book which is not returned according to the above rule. No book will be issued to any person incurring such a fine until it has been paid.
3. All injuries to books beyond reasonable wear and all losses shall be made good to the satisfaction of the Librarian.
4. Each borrower is held responsible for all books drawn on his card and for all fines accruing on the same.

THE MINNESOTA VIKINGS

JOHN F. GRABOWSKI

Other books in the Great Sports Teams series:

THE MINNESOTA VIKINGS

JOHN F. GRABOWSKI

LUCENT
BOOKS ®

THOMSON
★
™
GALE

San Diego • Detroit • New York • San Francisco • Cleveland
New Haven, Conn. • Waterville, Maine • London • Munich

THOMSON
─────✶─────   ™
GALE

796.332
GRA

On Cover: Vikings quarterback Daunte Culpepper scrambles for the sideline in 2001.

LIBRARY OF CONGRESS CATALOGING-IN-PUBLICATION DATA

Grabowski, John F.
    The Minnesota Vikings / by John F. Grabowski.
    p. cm. — (Great sports teams)
Summary: Discusses the history, formation, development, and popularity of the Min-
nesota Vikings football team, including a look at individual players who have had an
impact on the success of the team.
Includes bibliographical references and index.
    ISBN 1-56006-943-0 (hardback : alk. paper)
    1. Minnesota Vikings (Football team)—Juvenile literature. 2. Football players—
United States—Biography—Juvenile literature. [1. Minnesota Vikings (Football team)—
History. 2. Football—History. 3. Football players.] I. Title. II. Series: Great sports teams
(Lucent Books)
GV956.M5G73 2003
796.332'64'09776579—dc21
                                                                    2002012561

Printed in the United States of America

Contents

FOREWORD

Former Supreme Court Chief Justice Warren Burger once said he always read the sports section of the newspaper first because it was about humanity's successes, while the front page listed only humanity's failures. Millions of people across the country today would probably agree with Burger's preference for tales of human endurance, record-breaking performances, and feats of athletic prowess. Although these accomplishments are far beyond what most Americans can ever hope to achieve, average people, the fans, do want to affect what happens on the field of play. Thus, their role becomes one of encouragement. They cheer for their favorite players and team and boo the opposition.

ABC Sports president Roone Arledge once attempted to explain the relationship between fan and team. Sport, said Arledge, is "a set of created circumstances—artificial circumstances—set up to frustrate a man in pursuit of a goal. He has to have certain skills to overcome those obstacles—or even to challenge them. And people who don't have those skills cheer him and admire him." Over a period of time, the admirers may develop a rabid—even irrational—allegiance to a particular team. Indeed, the word "fan" itself is derived from the word "fanatic," someone possessed by an excessive and irrational zeal. Sometimes this devotion to a team is because of a favorite player; often it's because of where a person lives, and, occasionally, it's because of a family allegiance to a particular club.

Whatever the reason, the bond formed between team and fan often defies reason. It may be easy to understand the appeal of the New York Yankees, a team that has gone to the World Series an incredible thirty-eight times and won twenty-six championships, nearly three times as many as any other major league baseball team. It is more difficult, though, to comprehend the fanaticism of Chicago Cubs fans, who faithfully follow the progress of a team that has not won a World Series since 1908. Regardless, the Cubs have surpassed the 2 million mark in home attendance in fourteen of the last seventeen years. In fact, their two highest totals were posted in 1999 and 2000, when the team finished in last place.

Each volume in Lucent's Great Sports Teams series examines a team that has left its mark on the "American sports consciousness." Each book looks at the history and tradition of the club in an attempt to understand its appeal and the loyalty—even passion—of its fans. Each volume also examines the lives and careers of people who played significant roles in the team's history. Players, managers, coaches, and front-office executives are represented.

Endnoted quotations help bring the text in each book to life. In addition, all books include an annotated bibliography and a For Further Reading list to supply students with sources for conducting additional individual research.

No one volume can hope to explain fully the mystique of the New York Yankees, Boston Celtics, Dallas Cowboys, or Montreal Canadiens. The Lucent Great Sports Teams series, however, gives interested readers a solid start on the road to understanding the mysterious bond that exists between modern professional sports teams and their devoted followers.

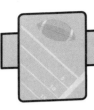

An Undeserved Reputation

The history of professional sports at the major-league level in the state of Minnesota is a relatively short one. Teams have come and gone over the years with varying degrees of success. Over the long haul, the Vikings have had the best overall record. In the past thirty-four years, they have had only six losing seasons and have won or tied for first in their division a remarkable sixteen times. Their failure to win a championship, however, has caused them to be looked upon as failures by much of the sporting community.

Champions and Also-Rans

The Minneapolis Lakers came into existence in 1947 and achieved quick success as the National Basketball Association's first dynasty. They won five NBA championships before the lure of greener pastures in California called them away in 1960. It was more than a quarter century before the Minnesota Timberwolves gave the region another basketball team to cheer for.

Hockey, arguably the most popular sport in the area, also lost a team to relocation. The Minnesota North Stars played in the National Hockey League from 1967 to 1993 before moving to

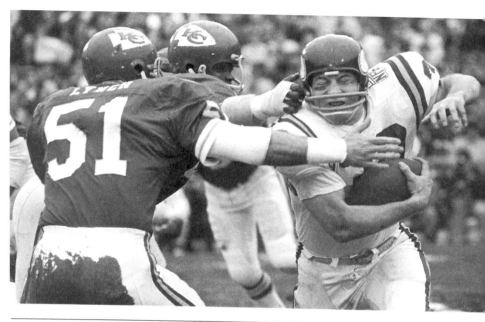

Vikings fullback Bill Brown (right) breaks a tackle in the first quarter of the 1970 Super Bowl.

Dallas and becoming the Stars. The expansion team Minnesota Wild was added to the league in 2000.

In baseball, the Washington Senators relocated to Minnesota in 1961 and were renamed the Minnesota Twins. Since then, they have won two world championships. Since 1977, however, they have spent more time than not in the bottom half of their division in the American League. Their future is uncertain, as they are one of the teams currently being considered for contraction in a sport considering possible solutions to its financial woes.

The Final Step

The Minnesota Vikings were added to the National Football League (NFL) mix in 1961, the same season as the Twins. They have won ten or more games in a season fourteen times in the last thirty-three years and had a streak of ten divisional titles in eleven years from 1968 through 1978. Since then, they have compiled the best winning percentage of Minnesota's six pro clubs, winning more than 55 percent of the games they have played in the regular season.

Sports fans and the media, however, generally equate success with championships. In this respect, the Vikings have been a failure. Although they have qualified for postseason play in more than 60 percent of their years in existence (an especially enviable record for a one-time expansion team), they have come up short in four appearances in the Super Bowl. Their 0–4 record in football's big game (matched only by the Buffalo Bills) has made them the object of ridicule and scorn. Such undeserved derision is the unfortunate plight of this proud franchise. Sadly, it will likely remain so until the day a championship banner flies above the Metrodome or some yet to be built stadium.

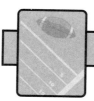

CHAPTER 1

Always a Bridesmaid

In the years since their inception in 1961, the Minnesota Vikings have experienced more success than many of their nonexpansion brethren. Only a handful of teams have appeared in the Super Bowl as many times as the Vikings. Most of those clubs, however, have won at least one championship. The only team to match Minnesota's record of four appearances and no wins is the Buffalo Bills. Sadly, rather than being praised for their overall record, the Vikings are often ridiculed for their failure to win football's ultimate game.

The Start of Something Big

In 1947, Austrian-born businessman Max Winter helped establish the Minneapolis (now Los Angeles) Lakers basketball team. During his term as general manager of the club, he had the opportunity to watch a National Football League (NFL) game in Chicago. He fell in love with the sport and decided to channel his energies into securing a franchise for the region. Winter began writing to the league asking for the chance to organize a new team, but was ignored.

Representatives from the newly founded American Football League pose for the camera in October 1959.

Together with local auto dealer William Boyer, he formed a group of five businessmen that included H.P. Skoglund, Bernard H. Ridder Jr., and Ole Haugsrud. (Haugsrud had owned the Duluth Eskimos in the early days of the NFL, but was forced to turn the franchise back over to the league.) The group first tried, unsuccessfully, to lure the Chicago Cardinals to the Twin Cities region of Minneapolis and St. Paul. In 1959, when the American Football League (AFL) came on the scene as a challenger to the older NFL, the group was prepared to accept an offer to become a charter member of the new circuit for $25,000.

Soon afterward, however, Winter received a letter from George Halas, head of the NFL expansion committee. He said the group would be granted an expansion franchise in the older league for a $50,000 fee, with the understanding they would not support the upstart AFL. They accepted the offer and began making plans to begin the 1961 season as the NFL's fourteenth team. (The AFL eventually replaced Minnesota with the Oakland Raiders.)

Winter, who was named the team's president, began searching for the right people to run his operation. He hired former

Los Angeles Rams public relations director Bert Rose as the team's general manager, and Joe Thomas as its main talent scout. It was Rose who came up with the team's name, suggesting Vikings because it represented an aggressive people with a strong will to succeed and the Nordic tradition of so many people living in the northern Midwest. In an announcement to the media about the team's name Winters said, "They say that the Norwegian Vikings were the first to discover America. Let's make Minnesota the first state to discover Viking football. Let's call them the Minnesota Vikings."[1]

Norm Van Brocklin, former Philadelphia Eagles quarterback, became the first coach of the Vikings in 1961.

Putting Together a Team

One of Rose's first jobs was to find a coach to lead his troops. He selected recently retired quarterback Norm Van Brocklin, who had just led the Philadelphia Eagles to the 1960 NFL title. Together, the pair faced a formidable task: to put together a team capable of competing with the more established NFL clubs. They took a major step by selecting Tulane running back Tommy Mason, Georgia quarterback Fran Tarkenton, and Pittsburgh cornerback Ed Sharockman, among others, in the 1961 college draft.

The league also held an expansion draft to help Minnesota fill out its roster. Each of the established teams (except second-year Dallas) was allowed to protect thirty of the thirty-eight men on their roster. The Vikings were then allowed to select three of the remaining players from each team for a total of thirty-six. Although most of those available were retreads and castoffs, the Vikings did acquire guard Grady Alderman and running back Hugh McElhenny in this way.

A final avenue left to the club for improvement was the trade route. The Vikings obtained veteran quarterback George Shaw in a deal with the New York Giants and defensive end Jim Marshall from the Cleveland Browns. Although the squad had some talented players, it still left much to be desired. As line coach Stan West said of his players, "They're not big, but they sure are slow."[2]

An Auspicious Debut

The Vikings were assigned to the NFL's Western Conference where they joined the Baltimore Colts, Chicago Bears, Detroit Lions, Green Bay Packers, Los Angeles Rams, and San Francisco 49ers. They took the field at the new Metropolitan Stadium in Bloomington on September 10, 1961, to face the Bears in the first regular season game in franchise history. With little expected of them, the Vikings pulled off a stunning upset, defeating Chicago by a score of 37–13 behind the heroics of rookie quarterback Tarkenton. Kicker Mike Mercer scored the team's first points on a field goal, and end Bob Schnelker scored the first touchdown in the club's history. As Van Brocklin said, "You can't ask for a better start than that."[3]

Unfortunately, the Vikings came back down to earth the following week, losing to Dallas, 21–7. They lost seven games in a row and finished the year with a record of 3–11. Despite the losing season, the following January, McElhenny and wide receiver Jerry Reichow became the first Vikings named to play in the Pro Bowl.

The team continued to strengthen itself over the next couple of seasons. Center Mick Tingelhoff was added as a free agent in 1962, and fullback Bill Brown and Rookie of the Year split end Paul Flatley in 1963. That year, Mason became the first Minnesota player to earn All-Pro recognition on the basis of his 763 yards gained rushing.

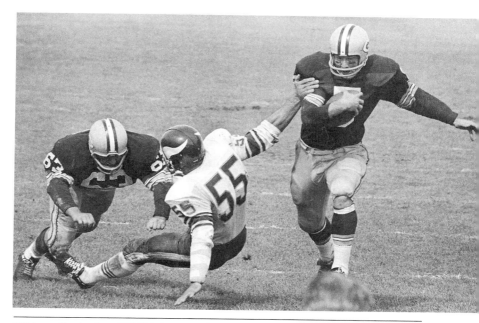

Vikings linebacker Cliff Livingston (55) tries in vain to stop the Green Bay Packers' Paul Hornung (right) in 1962.

A New Regime

Rose stepped down as general manager prior to the 1964 season. He was replaced by former Pittsburgh Steelers quarterback Jim Finks. Rookie end Carl Eller, drafted from the University of Minnesota, bolstered the team's defense. The Vikings won their final four games of the season and finished in a tie for second place in the Western Conference with their first winning record (8–5–1). Dissension was brewing, however, as Van Brocklin was becoming more and more disenchanted with Tarkenton's scrambling from the quarterback position, believing it to be an unnecessary risk.

In 1965, the Vikings fell to a disappointing 7–7 after being picked by many to contend for the conference title. When they lost to Baltimore in week 9, Van Brocklin had enough. He told reporters he was resigning, but changed his mind later that same day. He stayed the rest of the season, but matters only got worse.

The rift between Tarkenton and his coach continued to widen in 1966, a season in which the Vikings won just four games. Van Brocklin finally resigned the following February. In his place, Minnesota signed Harry "Bud" Grant, who had been a candidate for the original position back in 1961.

A Formidable Defense

Tarkenton was dealt to the New York Giants soon after Van Brocklin resigned, and Finks brought in Canadian Football League (CFL) star Joe Kapp to replace him. Grant then turned his attention toward improving the Minnesota defense. Over the next three years, he drafted defensive tackle Alan Page and cornerback Bobby Bryant. Defensive tackle Gary Larsen, linebacker Wally Hilgenberg, and free safety Paul Krause came to the Vikings through trades, and the defense known as the Purple People Eaters (because they played like monsters on defense) was born. (They were also called the Purple Gang.)

The defense consisted of Eller and Marshall at end, Larsen and Page at tackle, Hilgenberg at linebacker along with Roy Winston and Jeff Siemon, Bryant and Nate Wright at cornerback, and Krause and Jeff Wright at safety. The squad's objective was to "meet at the quarterback," in an attempt to sack him before he had a chance to throw the ball, and they did so with remarkable frequency. Over an eleven-year period, the Vikings averaged thirty-seven sacks per season.

The front four were the key to the defense. Although none weighed more than 250 pounds, they made up for it with their quickness and intelligence. As defensive line coach Jack Patera said, "What you look for is a man who plays big. If he can control his area at the line of scrimmage, he's big enough."[4] The Vikings certainly fit that description.

After a 3–8–3 year in 1967, the team followed up with its first NFL Central Division title the next season. They lost in the play-offs to the eventual NFL-champion Baltimore Colts. The next year, they rode a twelve-game winning streak to another division crown. They won the NFL title and faced the AFL-champion Kansas City Chiefs in Super Bowl IV. There, the Vikings were defeated, 23–7.

Though they lost the title, the Purple People Eaters led the NFL in fewest points allowed in 1969, 1970, and 1971. The 133 they surrendered in 1969 were the fewest ever given up in a fourteen-game schedule. In 1971, Page was named the Most Valuable Defensive Player in the NFL, and also won the Associated Press Most Valuable Player honors (the first time the award was ever won by a defensive tackle).

Tarkenton Returns

In 1972, the Vikings reacquired Tarkenton in a trade with the Giants. Tarkenton posted excellent statistics in his first year back, but the team struggled along to a 7–7 mark. The next year, Minnesota drafted running back Chuck Foreman in the first round of the college draft. His running added a new dimension to the club. The team got back on track and won in double digits in each of the next four seasons. With Tarkenton and Foreman leading the way, the squad reached the Super Bowl in three of those years.

Following the 1973 season, the Vikings met the defending Super Bowl champion Miami Dolphins in Super Bowl VIII. Tarkenton passed for more than twice as many yards as Miami's Bob Griese, but the Minnesota rushing attack was held in check. Foreman gained just eighteen yards in seven carries, and the Dolphins rolled to a 24–7 win.

The Vikings returned to the Super Bowl the next year when they met the Pittsburgh Steelers. In a battle of defenses, the Steelers prevailed, winning the first NFL championship in franchise history. Tarkenton threw three interceptions while Foreman again was held to less than twenty yards rushing.

The Hail Mary Pass

Minnesota had another powerhouse team in 1975 as Tarkenton was the National Football Conference's (NFC) leading passer. Foreman gained over one thousand yards on the ground for the first of three consecutive years, just missing the conference rushing title by six yards. The Vikings fell shy of the Super Bowl, however, when they were defeated by the Dallas Cowboys in the NFC divisional play-off on Roger Staubach's famous Hail Mary pass.

With less than two minutes remaining in the contest, Minnesota took a 14–10 lead on a one-yard plunge by Brent McClanahan. Dallas got the ball back on their own fifteen-yard line, and quarterback Staubach started moving them down the field. They got to midfield with less than thirty seconds left on the clock and no time-outs remaining. On the next play, Staubach tossed a bomb in the direction of wide receiver Drew Pearson, who was being covered by Nate Wright. As the players leaped for the ball, Pearson appeared to push off Wright and catch the pass against his hip at the five-yard line. He made it into the end zone with the winning score, depriving the Vikings of their third straight appearance in the Super Bowl. After the game, Staubach described the play to reporters, saying, "It was just a Hail Mary pass; a very, very lucky play."[5]

As Vikings defender Nate Wright (43) falls to the turf, Cowboys wide receiver Drew Pearson (88) descends into the end zone in the final play of the 1975 Super Bowl.

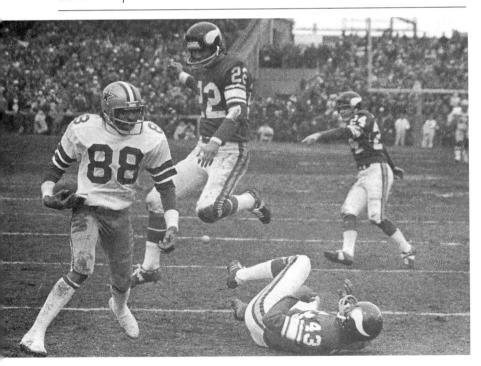

Another Super Bowl Disappointment

The Vikings bounced back strong in 1976, determined to gain revenge for their play-off loss at the hands of the Cowboys. Minnesota compiled an 11–2–1 record in a season highlighted by numerous individual milestones. Quarterback Tarkenton surpassed three thousand career completions, forty thousand yards passing, and three hundred touchdown passes while completing an NFC-high 61.9 percent of his throws. Running back Chuck Foreman rushed for a Minnesota-record two hundred yards in a game against the Philadelphia Eagles, and defensive end Jim Marshall surpassed George Blanda's NFL record for consecutive games played.

When the Vikings defeated the Green Bay Packers, 17–10, on November 21, they clinched their fourth consecutive NFC Central Division championship, and eighth division title in nine years. Minnesota raced through the play-offs, overwhelming the Washington Redskins (35–20) and Los Angeles Rams (24–13) to make it to their fourth Super Bowl.

On January 9, 1977, the Vikings took the field against the Oakland Raiders before a record Super Bowl crowd of 103,438 at the Rose Bowl in Pasadena, California. More than 81 million television viewers also tuned in, the largest audience ever for a sporting event. The first quarter was a defensive battle that ended in a scoreless tie. The Raiders, however, scored sixteen unanswered points in the second quarter, and the Vikings could not dig themselves out of the hole. The final score was Oakland thirty-two, Minnesota fourteen, as the Vikings lost their record fourth Super Bowl.

Despite the disappointment of the loss, Tarkenton continued to remain upbeat. As he said after the game, "We're gonna keep coming back until we find an AFC [American Football Conference] team we can beat."[6]

Other players, however, were harder to console. As linebacker Jeff Siemon explained, "With all the winning we'd done in the last ten years, [the loss] was impossible to swallow. I don't really know why we played so badly."[7] What neither player knew was that they would never again play for football's ultimate prize.

*Vikings wide receiver Sammy White retains the ball despite having his
helmet knocked off in a tackle by two Raiders backs in the 1977 Super Bowl.*

A Period of Transition

Over the next couple of years, the Vikings dropped out of the
league's upper echelon of teams. They did manage to make it
back to the NFC championship game in 1977, even though they
lost five games during the regular season. The eventual Super
Bowl champion Dallas Cowboys soundly defeated them by a
score of 23–6 to cut short their dreams of a title.

In 1978, an aging Minnesota squad made it to the play-offs
with an 8–7–1 record, but lost to the Rams in the opening
round. The following year, they finished the regular season
with a losing record (7–9) for the first time since 1967.

By the time 1980 rolled around, the club had undergone significant changes. Viking veterans Tarkenton, Page, Eller, Tingelhoff,
Marshall, Hilgenberg, and Krause were all gone from the roster,
either having retired or been released. Star running back Chuck
Foreman would join the list before the start of the 1980 season.

The young team was now in the hands of Tommy Kramer, who had taken over as quarterback when Tarkenton retired following the 1978 season. Kramer's two main receivers were Ahmad Rashad (who led the NFC in receptions in 1977 and 1979) and Sammy White (the NFC Rookie of the Year in 1976). It would not be long before Kramer and Rashad combined on one of the most memorable plays in Vikings history.

Another Hail Mary

The Vikings started out slowly in 1980, but Kramer soon had them back in contention for the play-offs. Over the second half of the year, the team played solid fundamental football. By the time they faced the Cleveland Browns on December 14, 1980, the Vikings were in first place in the Central Division.

Kramer takes the snap, setting up the legendary 1980 Hail Mary play that became one of the most memorable in Vikings history.

With time running out in the game, a Cleveland field goal put the Vikings on the short end of a 23–22 score. Following a touchback on the ensuing kickoff, Minnesota took over on its own twenty-yard line with just twelve seconds left on the clock.

On the next play, Kramer took the snap from center and tossed a short pass to tight end Joe Senser. Senser caught the ball and immediately lateraled to running back Ted Brown who galloped down the field before going out of bounds at the Cleveland forty-seven yard line. With time for just one more play, the Vikings lined up for a Hail Mary pass in a formation known as Squadron Right. Kramer took the snap, and Rashad, White, and wide receiver Terry LeCount all headed for the end zone. Kramer heaved the ball where the three receivers and a half dozen Cleveland defenders were all converging. As the players jumped for it, the ball was tipped into the air. Rashad reached up to grab it and pull it in just as he backed into the end zone. Metropolitan Stadium erupted in a roar as the crowd realized what had happened. The Vikings had clinched a play-off spot on one of the greatest plays in team history.

Unfortunately, the team could not carry that good feeling over into the play-offs. Leading the Philadelphia Eagles 14–0 in the NFC division play-off, the Vikings fell apart in the second half of the game and came out on the short end of a 31–16 score.

The 1980s

Minnesota struggled through the first half of the decade, compiling a winning record only once over the next five years. That was in the strike-shortened 1982 season, when the club began playing in the new Hubert H. Humphrey Metrodome. After an 8–8 record in 1983, however, coach Bud Grant announced his retirement. He was replaced by Les Steckel.

Under Steckel, the Vikings lost a franchise-worst thirteen games in 1984. Grant returned in 1985, but retired for good after one year. He stepped down as the sixth winningest coach in league history with 168 career wins, including play-offs. He turned over control of the team to his longtime assistant Jerry Burns.

Burns produced four straight winning teams in Minnesota, but no conference champions. The closest he came was in 1987. After upsetting the New Orleans Saints and San Francisco 49ers in the first two rounds of the play-offs, the Vikings played the Washington Redskins in the NFC championship game. Trailing 17–10 with a little over a minute left in the contest, Minnesota had the ball on the Washington six-yard line. They could not push the ball across for the tying touchdown, however, and returned home to watch the Redskins defeat the Denver Broncos in Super Bowl XXII.

Burns was coach in 1989 when Vikings' general manager Mike Lynn engineered a trade that helped speed up the Vikings' decline and was a key factor in the rise of the Dallas Cowboys. Believing the Vikings to be in need of a top-quality running back in order to return to the Super Bowl, Lynn acquired All-Pro fullback Herschel Walker and four draft picks from Dallas in exchange for five roster players (defensive back Issiac Holt, linebackers David Howard and Jesse Solomon, running back Darrin Nelson, and defensive end Alex Stewart) and six draft picks, making it the largest trade in NFL history. Wise use of the draft picks enabled the Cowboys to build a club that would win consecutive Super Bowls in 1993 and 1994. The Vikings, meanwhile, reversed their 10–6 record of 1989 and fell into the NFC Central Division cellar in 1990. Lynn became the most hated man in Minnesota annals, and Walker was gone by the beginning of the 1992 season.

Enter Dennis Green

On New Year's Day 1991, Roger Headrick became president and chief executive officer of the Vikings. He took over the day-to-day operations of the team from Mike Lynn. When Burns retired following the 1991 season, former Stanford University coach Dennis Green was hired as his successor. Green became the second black head coach in NFL history.

The Vikings responded to the change in leadership by winning the Central Division title with a record of 11–5. Second-year running back Terry Allen led the club, rushing for more than twelve hundred yards. The eleven wins were the most by a first-year head coach in the team's history. Unfortunately, the Vikings could not get past the Redskins in the NFC wild card game, bringing their season to an end.

Over the first nine years of Green's tenure, the Vikings did not have a single losing season. In addition to 1992, the team made the play-offs in 1993, 1994, 1996, 1997, 1998 (when they finished with a 15–1 record, the best mark in franchise history), 1999, and 2000. Unfortunately, however, the club could not make it past the NFC championship game. Despite his overall success, Green's failure to guide the club into the Super Bowl was seen by many as an unforgivable sin.

Perhaps their hardest loss of all was to the Atlanta Falcons in the 1998 NFC championship game. The heavily favored Vikings jumped out to a 20–7 lead and were in front, 27–20, with the ball on Atlanta's twenty-nine-yard line and just 2:11 remaining in regulation time. Minnesota kicker Gary Anderson lined up for a thirty-eight-yard field goal that would clinch the victory. Despite the fact that Anderson had not missed a kick all year, he blew this one, giving the Falcons a chance to tie the score. After doing so, Atlanta went on to score a game-winning field goal eleven minutes and fifty-two seconds into the sudden-death overtime period.

Tragedy Strikes

The loss to Atlanta, however, seemed meaningless compared to a loss suffered in 2001. During training camp prior to the 2001

Minnesota's Gary Anderson (1) shanks a kick, missing a field goal in the 1998 NFC championship game against the Atlanta Falcons.

regular season, Minnesota's Pro Bowl offensive tackle Korey Stringer collapsed and died of heatstroke. The team never seemed to recover from the tragedy. Wide receiver Randy Moss alienated many players on the team with his admission that he did not play at full speed at all times. When Green failed to admonish him, it appeared that he was losing control of the team. With the Vikings' record at 5–10 with one game left in the regular season, the club bought out the rest of Green's contract. He was replaced by former tight end and offensive line coach Mike Tice.

Vikings coach Dennis Green announces that he is no longer the team's coach in January 2002.

Despite the fact that the Vikings have been one of the NFL's most successful franchises over the past forty years, their future is uncertain. How they perform on the field will depend in large part on how Tice handles enigmatic star receiver Moss.

Off the field, owner Red McCombs, who bought the franchise in 1998, has been dropping hints that he may sell the team, or relocate to Los Angeles or San Antonio. Despite selling out all their home games, the Vikings ranked next to last in 2001 in local revenues. This is due to the failure of the Metrodome to provide as much revenue from concessions, luxury seating, and parking as other more modern stadiums. McCombs has approached the Minnesota legislature seeking state help for the construction of a new stadium.

Minnesota governor Jesse Ventura has vowed to fight any proposed move. With the club having a lease that runs through 2011, Minnesotans hope the team will remain in the region long enough to win that elusive Super Bowl championship.

CHAPTER 2

Fran Tarkenton

Quarterback Fran Tarkenton failed to win a Super Bowl in three shots at football's top prize. He did, however, set numerous passing records in his career, a career that saw him thrill millions of fans with his daring scampers while avoiding the clutches of opposing linemen. More than any other player, he made scrambling an acceptable offensive option for quarterbacks. Many observers considered him one of the best quarterbacks ever to play the game.

A Religious Upbringing

Francis Asbury Tarkenton was born on February 3, 1940, in Richmond, Virginia. He was the son of the Reverend Dallas Tarkenton, a preacher in the Pentecostal Church, and his wife, Frances. The Tarkentons named their son after a missionary who was known as the "Father of American Methodism."

Fran and his two brothers, Dallas Jr. and Wendell, were raised in a strict home, where smoking, drinking, and cursing were not allowed. Playing sports was acceptable, however. When Fran was five, his family moved to Washington, D.C., where he was introduced to football. He played pickup games with the neighborhood kids and demonstrated a fierce will to win and a quick temper at an early age.

On one occasion, young Fran became particularly frustrated with his older brother Dallas's athletic superiority. He took a butcher's knife and chased his brother through the streets. Later, he would recall, "I still can't stand to lose, but I think I learned something from that experience. I didn't know it then, but I came to realize that losing my temper wouldn't get me anywhere."[8]

As a boy of ten, Fran played end with the Merrick Boys Club team in Washington. His dream, however, was to play quarterback like his hero, Washington Redskins star Sammy Baugh. Soon afterward, he got his chance. The family moved to Athens, Georgia in 1951 and Fran won the quarterback job with the Athens YMCA boys' team. By this time, he had made up his mind that he was going to be a professional athlete when he grew up.

When Fran entered Athens High School, he won the starting quarterback job as a five-foot, ten-inch, 150-pound freshman. His coach was an old-fashioned taskmaster named Weyman Sellers. Sellers's legendary practices were tougher than those of anyone else, but helped the teenager mature as a player. As he later admitted in his biography, "Most of what I still use I got from the Athens High School Trojans and Weyman Sellers."[9]

As a junior, Fran took the undefeated Trojans to the Georgia state finals. In the championship game against Valdosta High School, he ran the opening kickoff back for a touchdown. When the officials nullified the play because of a penalty, he repeated the feat, returning the ensuing kickoff ninety-nine yards for a score. Athens went on to win the title, 41–20, a remarkable feat considering that Fran had played the entire season with a badly separated shoulder.

Fran's senior season at Athens was a disappointment. The club lost many of its players to graduation and could not repeat its success of the previous year. Despite this, Fran still received several scholarship offers, finally deciding to stay in Athens and play at the University of Georgia.

A Bulldog All-American

Playing for the freshman team at Georgia, Tarkenton's confidence was rebuilt by coach Quinton Lumkin. By the time he moved up to coach Wally Butts's varsity team as a sophomore in 1958, he was ready to show what he could do. He began the season as the third-string quarterback.

In the Bulldogs' opening game against the Texas Longhorns, Georgia trailed, 7–0, in the third quarter. With the offense going nowhere, Tarkenton pleaded with Butts on the sideline, "I can do it, I can get you a touchdown in this game, I can get this thing going."[10] Butts ignored him as the game progressed. When Georgia regained possession of the ball a short time later, Tarkenton decided to take matters into his own hands. He ran onto the field, making believe he did not hear his coach calling after him. He proceeded to lead the Bulldogs ninety-five yards down the field to a touchdown that gave them an 8–7 lead. Butts, furious that Tarkenton had gone in without receiving permission, benched him for the remainder of the game. Georgia went on to lose, but the quarterback had learned a valuable lesson: If he was to become a leader, he had to learn to follow directions. Tarkenton learned his lesson well. By the middle of the season, he was the starting quarterback. The next year, he was named an All–Southeastern Conference selection as a junior.

Fran Tarkenton became the starting quarterback for the Georgia Bulldogs his sophomore year.

Tarkenton was a preseason All-American choice in 1960, but his size had NFL scouts leery about his chances for success as a pro. Now six-foot, one-inch tall and 190 pounds, he was still small for a quarterback by NFL standards. Tarkenton, however, had confidence in his abilities. "I don't think Coach Butts thinks I can make it in the pros," he said. "I'm going to prove them all wrong."[11] He would get his chance with the Minnesota Vikings, an expansion team that selected him in the third round of the 1961 NFL draft.

An Impressive Debut

Tarkenton's first pro contract called for a salary of $12,500 and a $3,500 bonus. The team he joined was for the most part a collection of NFL rejects and has-beens selected in the expansion draft. However, added to the mix via the college draft was another future star in running back Tommy Mason. The coach of the team was Hall of Fame quarterback Norm Van Brocklin.

Tarkenton began the Vikings' first training camp as the second-string quarterback behind veteran George Shaw. The rookie impressed Van Brocklin with his play, but he chose Shaw to start in the first game of the season against the Chicago Bears. The first quarter was not over, however, when Tarkenton went in to replace Shaw.

What happened over the remainder of the game shocked the Bears as well as much of the pro football world. In one of the greatest debuts by a quarterback in league history, Tarkenton completed seventeen of twenty-three passes for 250 yards and four touchdowns. For good measure, he ran for another touchdown himself. The Vikings upset the Bears, winning their first regular-season game ever by a score of 37–13.

The Scrambler

Reality set in for Minnesota the following week, however, and the Vikings lost their next seven games. They finished the year with a record of three wins and eleven defeats. A major reason for the team's poor showing was its weak offensive line. Defensive linemen found little resistance as they made their way into the backfield where they battered Tarkenton time and time again. His only option was to scramble, or run around behind the line of scrimmage dodging would-be tacklers, when his receivers were covered, and the protective pocket around him

Tarkenton (10) rushes for a touchdown against the Chicago Bears in 1973.

broke down. By doing this, he rushed for 308 yards and a career-high five touchdowns.

The scrambling, however, did not sit well with the coach. "When a quarterback is forced to run," explained Van Brocklin, "you have taken away his effectiveness and made him play your game. He won't beat you running. He'll beat you throwing the ball. That's what he's paid to do. . . . He should run only from sheer terror."[12]

In 1962, the Vikings won just two games as Tarkenton suffered through his worst season. His scrambling was more productive (361 yards), but his passing completion percentage was a career-low 49.5 percent. He also threw twenty-five interceptions.

It would be another year before Tarkenton began to feel like he was coming into his own as a quarterback. "It wasn't until [1963] that I felt that I was beginning to be a genuine, bona fide professional quarterback," he said, "able to react properly to the pressures of the game. That's the dominating factor about pro football, the pressure, and you can't stay around if you can't handle it."[13] In leading Minnesota to a 5–8 mark, he finished sixth among NFL passers.

In 1964, Tarkenton led the Vikings to their first-ever winning season. By this time, the fans and media were calling him the "Scrambler." In a game against the Green Bay Packers in early October, he added to this reputation. With the Vikings trailing, 23–21, and with time running out, Minnesota had fourth down and twenty-two yards to go. In the huddle, Tarkenton addressed his receivers. "We've got to do something drastic," he said. "All you receivers run down field twenty-five yards. I'll scramble around until I find one of you open."[14]

The play was a success as Gordie Smith caught the desperation throw for a first down. It marked the first time Tarkenton actually called a scramble as a play. The Vikings went on to score a field goal to give them a 24–23 victory.

In guiding the team to eight wins in fourteen games that year, Tarkenton finished second among quarterbacks to Green Bay's Bart Starr with a rating of 91.8. He also rushed for 330 yards on the ground. By this time, Van Brocklin had resigned himself to Tarkenton's scrambling ways. "I tried to make him stand in there," said the former quarterback, "but once we accepted what he was, we decided to live with it. . . . It was appealing and it was successful for a while."[15] It would not be long, however, before Van Brocklin had enough.

Tarkenton scrambles to find an open receiver in a 1964 game against the Packers.

On to New York

The Vikings dropped back to .500 in 1965 with a 7–7 mark. The next year, they fell into a tie for last place in the NFL Western Conference with four wins, nine losses, and one tie. Tarkenton's scrambling accounted for 356 yards in 1965 and a career-high 376 the next year. His passing ratings, however, fell to 83.8 and 73.8 over that same time.

Relations between Tarkenton and his coach continued to deteriorate. They reached a low point when Van Brocklin benched him in favor of backup quarterback Bob Berry in a game against the Atlanta Falcons.

In addition to his negative feelings about scrambling, Van Brocklin had a mercurial temper. He felt some players on the team were trying to undermine his authority and did not hesitate to accuse others of selfishness, laziness, stupidity, and cowardice. His actions turned most of the players against him.

After the 1966 season, Tarkenton had had enough. On February 10, he sent Van Brocklin a letter of resignation in an attempt to force a trade to another team. "After much thought," he wrote, "I have come to a definite conclusion that under no circumstances can I return to play football with the Minnesota Vikings next season."[16]

The Minnesota front office was upset, believing that Tarkenton was trying to force them to fire Van Brocklin. When the Dutchman himself resigned two days later, many thought Tarkenton would reconsider his position. He did not, however, and on March 7, he was sent to the New York Giants in exchange for three draft choices.

Rebuilding the Giants

After having experienced much success in the 1950s and early 1960s, the Giants had fallen on hard times. They finished the 1966 season with a record of 1–12–1, the worst mark in the NFL. Tarkenton helped them return to mediocrity, if not respectability. In his first four seasons with the team, the Giants compiled a record of twenty-nine wins and twenty-seven losses. Although he received criticism from some who considered him nothing more than a .500 quarterback, the players

As quarterback of the New York Giants, Tarkenton managed to lead the team to four consecutive second-place finishes.

knew otherwise. "In a couple of those seasons," said Giants center Greg Larson, "we wouldn't have won a game without Tarkenton."[17]

In 1967, Tarkenton threw for over three thousand yards in the air and completed a career-high twenty-nine passes for touchdowns while finishing third among league passers. He did not reach those heights again, but did manage to guide New York to four consecutive second-place finishes in its division.

In 1971, the Giants dropped to 4–10. The thirty-two-year-old Tarkenton sensed that it was time for him to move on once again. The Giants accommodated him with a trade back to Minnesota. The team he returned to, however, was a different one from the one he had left in 1967.

Super Disappointments

Bud Grant had molded the Vikings into one of the NFL's dominant teams. The club had won four consecutive division crowns, and made it all the way to Super Bowl IV in 1970. There, they had lost to the Kansas City Chiefs, 23–7. Grant hoped Tarkenton would be the one to get them past that final hurdle and bring a championship to Minnesota. Success was not immediate, however. The Vikings were just 7–7 in 1972, finishing out of the play-offs.

The following season, Tarkenton led the team to a 12–2 record to tie the Los Angeles Rams for the best mark in the conference. They defeated Washington and Dallas in the play-offs

Tarkenton (10) faces a tough Pittsburgh Steelers defense during Super Bowl IX in 1975.

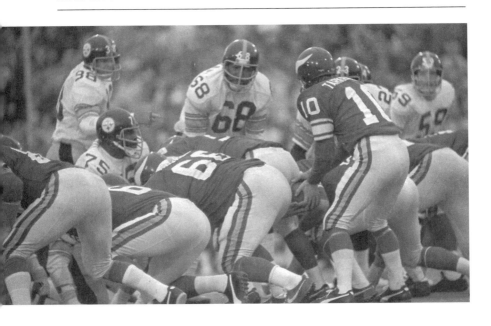

to reach Super Bowl VII. Minnesota's fun finally ended when they were defeated by the Miami Dolphins, 24–7.

Tarkenton and the Vikings put together another magnificent season in 1974, again reaching the Super Bowl. This time, they were cut down by the powerful Pittsburgh Steelers of Terry Bradshaw and Mean Joe Greene. Tarkenton's frustration was beginning to show. "I wanted to win a championship desperately," he said. "It's probably what I want more than anything in the world."[18]

The following spring, Max Winter took over active management of the Minnesota franchise. Mike Lynn took over as the club's new general manager. Tarkenton responded by having one of his best all-around seasons. He guided the Vikings to another 12–2 record while leading the NFC in passing with a 91.7 rating. He accounted for nearly three thousand yards through the air and passed for twenty-five touchdowns. His performance was recognized when he was awarded the Jim Thorpe Trophy as the NFL's Most Valuable Player.

In the play-offs, however, Minnesota's season was ruined in the NFC championship game. With just twenty-four seconds remaining in the contest, the Dallas Cowboys scored a touchdown on Roger Staubach's famous fifty-yard Hail Mary pass to end Drew Pearson. Despite Minnesota's vehement protest that the Cowboys had committed interference on the play, the officals refused to recognize it. The Cowboys won, 17–14, and advanced to the Super Bowl. The Vikings' loss took on tragic overtones for Tarkenton when he learned after the game that his father had died while watching the contest on television at home in Minnesota.

Bent on revenge, the Vikings raced through the 1976 season with a conference-best 11–2–1 record. They did not face the Cowboys in the play-offs, but made it to the Super Bowl for the third time in four years. Their opponent this time was the AFC-champion Oakland Raiders of coach John Madden. A title was not meant to be, however. The Vikings fell to Oakland, 32–14, for an unprecedented fourth Super Bowl loss.

Playing Out the String

Tarkenton led Minnesota into the postseason in both 1977 and 1978 as the team won its ninth and tenth division titles in an eleven-year span. They could not make it back to the Super Bowl, however, losing to Dallas in the NFC championship game in 1977, and to Los Angeles in the NFC divisional play-offs the following season.

Prior to the start of the 1978 season, Tarkenton had made up his mind that it would be his last year, win or lose. "I've played this game since I was eleven years old," he said. "I don't want to hang around for a paycheck. You wake up and you're thirty-nine and you know it's time to move on."[19]

Following the loss to the Rams, he formally announced his retirement. Tributes immediately began to pour in from team-mates and opponents alike. "To get to play on the same team with him, work with him, catch passes from him—that's been like a dream," said teammate Ahmad Rashad. "I hate to see him quit. There'll be a void here and in the whole NFL."[20]

Never one to rest on his laurels, Tarkenton moved on to become a successful businessman in his adopted hometown of Atlanta, Georgia, where he was founder and chairman of the board of Tarkenton & Co. He tried his hand at television as a football broadcaster, but is perhaps most famous as being one of the cohosts of *That's Incredible* with John Davidson and Cathy Lee Crosby. He has also donated much of his time to charitable organizations such as the Diabetes Foundation and the Viking Children's Fund.

Today Tarkenton is a successful entrepreneur. He has run a dozen different businesses that have earned more than $100 million in annual revenues. He manages the Fran Tarkenton Small Business Network, which helps countless small businesses throughout the country by offering various services. Tarkenton is also a motivational speaker and the author of *What Losing Taught Me About Winning*.

After eighteen NFL seasons, Tarkenton retired as the league's all-time leader in pass completions, passing yardage, and touchdown passes. Tarkenton was elected to the Pro Football Hall of Fame in 1986. Although he never won football's biggest prize, he was still called by Bud Grant "the greatest quarterback ever to play the game."[21]

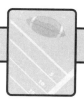

CHAPTER 3

Jim Marshall

Jim Marshall was the Lou Gehrig and Cal Ripken of the National Football League. He played an incredible 282 consecutive games—302 including play-offs—over the course of twenty seasons. One of the team's cocaptains, he was an important member of the Purple People Eaters defense of the late 1960s.

The Value of Dedication

James Lawrence Marshall was born in Danville, Kentucky, on December 30, 1937. He grew up in a poor neighborhood, but was lucky to have a family that stressed the importance of an education and strong values. He grew up with an understanding of what it meant to work toward a goal. As he later explained, "When I make a commitment to do something, I do it. It's the foundation for the way I live my life. My father and grandfather advocated the importance of commitments. A commitment, that's your work, your bond."[22]

Jim had a rich fantasy life as a youngster. He dreamed of being an astronaut, a mountain climber, a deep-sea diver, a sky diver, and an explorer. One of his dreams was to be a

professional football player. At East High School in Colum-
bus, Ohio, Jim committed himself to the sport. He was a
member of two undefeated teams during his high school career, and won many accolades for his play as a lineman.
Among these were All-City, All-State, and All-American honors. He also played in the High School All-Star Game as a senior. When it came time to choose a college, Jim elected to
stay near home and attend Ohio State University (OSU).

At OSU, Jim played tackle under legendary coach Woody
Hayes, and also starred in track. Over the course of Marshall's
seasons under Hayes, the Buckeyes won a National Championship (1957) and a Rose Bowl (1958). Marshall starred at defensive tackle and earned All-American honors in 1958 when
he teamed up with future pros Jim Houston, Dick Schafrath,
and Jim Tyrer to form one of the greatest lines in college history. For his performance on the field, he was eventually
elected to both the Ohio State University Hall of Fame and the
College Football Hall of Fame.

Arguably the greatest game of his career came against Big
Ten rival Purdue in 1958. Ohio State tied the Boilermakers,
14–14, as Marshall accounted for all his team's points. He
scored one touchdown on an intercepted pass and another on
a recovered fumble after a blocked punt. He also kicked both
extra points.

A Career in the Pros

Marshall passed up his senior season and left school a year
early to play in the Canadian Football League for the
Saskatchewan Roughriders in 1959. (He could not play in the
NFL, since his class had not yet graduated.) The next year, he
joined the Cleveland Browns, who drafted him in the fourth
round (the forty-fourth overall pick) of the 1960 NFL draft. (He
was also selected by the Houston Oilers of the new American
Football League in the league's first draft that year.) By this
time, his position had been switched to defensive end.

Marshall played his first game for the Browns on September
25, 1960, against the Philadelphia Eagles. "I was underweight,"
he recalled, "recovering from encephalitis and so nervous
about it I didn't want my wife [at the time his fiancée] to come

watch. I didn't invite her to the game because I wasn't sure I'd play well, and I didn't want her to see me play bad."[23] Despite his illness, he started all twelve games for the 8–3–1 Browns that season.

In part because of the encephalitis that weakened him and caused him to lose weight, the Browns sent Marshall to the expansion Minnesota Vikings as part of an eight-player trade prior to the start of the next season (August 31, 1961). In addition to Marshall, Minnesota received tackle Paul Dickson, fullback Jamie Caleb, defensive tackle Jim Prestel, linebacker Dick Grecni, and defensive back Bill Gault. In return, the Browns received two 1962 draft choices who turned

Jim Marshall (70) closes in on Baltimore's Johnny Unitas.

out to be defensive tackle Charles Hinton and end Ronnie Myers. The deal turned out to be a steal for the Vikings. In addition to Marshall (who would play nineteen years with the team), both Dickson and Prestel became starters. The other three players each spent a season with Minnesota. Neither of the players the Browns drafted ever played a down with the team.

Marshall quickly established himself as one of the league's top defensive ends. Though small for his position, his speed helped him burst past opposing linemen. He gave one-hundred percent of himself on every play, game after game. His zest for the game knew no bounds.

Marshall brought with him the kind of attitude that would endear him to any coach. "The greatest thing about Marshall," said Vikings' coach Bud Grant, "is that he never let the game get away from the playground. He's not the shrewdest player, but he wasn't constructed that way. He learned the game believing there's no problem that can't be overcome if you run at it hard enough."[24] He would face one such problem midway through the 1964 season.

The Wrong-Way Run

On October 25, 1964, the Vikings and San Francisco 49ers met at Kezar Stadium in San Francisco. The game was won by Minnesota, 27–22, but the final score was not much more than an afterthought to the thousands of fans who witnessed the contest. For them, it will always be remembered as the day of the NFL's most famous blooper, Jim Marshall's wrong-way run.

With the Vikings leading, 20–17, in the fourth quarter, Marshall hit Niner quarterback George Mira, forcing a fumble. Marshall's teammate, Carl Eller, picked up the ball and rambled into the end zone with it for a touchdown and a 27–17 Minnesota lead.

That was the way the score stood with just over eight minutes left in the game. With the 49ers on the offensive, Mira completed a pass to Billy Kilmer who dropped the ball when he was hit. Marshall picked it up at San Francisco's thirty-four-yard line, spun around, and began heading for the end zone. "I picked it up and took off running," recalled Marshall. "Everyone was waving and shouting, but I thought they were cheering me on."[25]

Unfortunately, such was not the case. They were yelling, as it turned out, because Marshall was heading toward his own end zone. Sixty-six yards later, he heaved the ball into the air, believing he had scored a touchdown. "What alerted me that something was wrong was the noise," said Marshall. "I had never heard a crowd react that way. Then I turned and saw some of my teammates pointing back the other way. [49er center] Bruce Bosley grabbed me and said thanks. My spirits just sank."[26] Rather than giving the Vikings an almost insurmountable lead, the safety resulted in two points for San Francisco. A 49er's field goal finished the scoring, giving Minnesota a 27-22 victory.

Sadly, despite Marshall's years of inspirational play for the Vikings, most fans immediately think of his wrong-way run when his name is brought up. More astute observers of the game, however, recognized his importance to the team. "I thought Marshall was the most complete player in the sense that he did it all," said Paul Wiggins, the Vikings' personnel director. "He was a topnotch pass rusher, a topnotch run defender, an all-out player. He didn't pick his spots. He played hard all the time. He had all the things you love in a player."[27]

The Purple People Eaters

With the Vikings, Marshall became a key player on the team's Purple People Eaters defensive line. The line featured Carl Eller at left defensive end, Gary Larsen next to him at left defensive tackle, Alan Page at right defensive tackle, and Marshall at right defensive end. The quartet was smaller than other units, like the Rams' Fearsome Foursome, but made up for their lack of size with exceptional speed and quickness. Time after time, the group sacked quarterbacks, forced fumbles, blocked punts, and made plays that could turn defeat into victory in the blink of an eye.

Hall of Fame quarterback Johnny Unitas of the Baltimore Colts called Minnesota's linemen the best pass rushers he had ever seen. The number of sacks they recorded was just a small measure of their effect on the game. "The most important point in rushing the passer," said Minnesota's defensive line coach Jack Patera, "is not how often you dump him, but how much pressure you put on him. The job of a defensive line is to collapse the

The Purple People Eaters: (from left to right) Jim Marshall, Alan Page, Carl Eller, and Gary Larsen.

pocket on a quarterback and crowd him into inaccuracy. If you do this correctly, the sacks will take care of themselves."[28]

As a group, the Purple People Eaters revolutionized defensive play in the NFL. "At our peak," said Marshall proudly, "we changed the game. Rules were passed to help teams adjust to us. The new holding rules, the outlawing of the head slap—that was because of the things we did. We were like a SWAT team, a strike task force—quick and agile. Apart, we were entirely different, but put us together and we clicked. It got to the point where I knew what the others were going to do the moment they started it. It was just understood."[29]

The Streak

In 1975, Marshall played in his 225th consecutive game to set a new NFL iron-man record. He amazed everyone with his ability to play at a high level week after week. The following season, coach Grant recounted one of his performances against the Los Angeles Rams. Describing the game films, Grant said,

> You'd see a thirty-eight year old man going full bore from start to finish against one of the best teams in football, and not only against the man assigned to block him. They had a rookie quarterback [Pat Haden] so they gave him maximum protection by doubling on our defensive ends. They had a 270-pound tackle and a 230-pound fullback blocking on Marshall. I don't know how many times he shook those blocks and ran the width of the field chasing a play. You have to be in football to know how much that takes out of a man. We substituted for practically everybody on the defensive team, but Marshall was still going wide open at the finish.

Marshall cracks a smile during his record-setting 225th consecutive NFL game.

Buddy Ryan, our defensive coach, has seen a lot of great players over the years. He came up to me after the game. He said, "I can't believe this guy. I never saw anybody like him."[30]

Even illnesses and injuries could not keep Marshall out of the lineup. His streak almost ended once when he was hospitalized with a case of acute asthmatic bronchitis. Despite being in an oxygen tent during the week, he could not be kept away from the game on Sunday. "I took the tubes out," he remembered, "and, all of a sudden, I showed up for the game. And I played every down."[31]

Marshall himself gave Vikings' trainer Fred Zamberletti much of the credit for his durability. "Fred Zamberletti shares in that record as much as I do," he said. "He kept me healthy for 19 seasons."[32]

Oddly enough, although Marshall was able to avoid streak-ending injuries and diseases, he was not as lucky during the off-season. Included among his brushes with death and dismemberment were a self-inflicted gunshot wound, a crash of a motorized hang glider, internal bleeding requiring surgery following a tonsillectomy, several automobile accidents, an incident in the early sixties when he almost choked to death on a grape, and a blizzard during a snowmobiling expedition in Wyoming. The last in the list occurred in 1970 in the Beartooth Mountains. The blizzard hit his sixteen-man party, forcing them to make their way down through the snow in darkness. One man died along the way, but Marshall and the others survived.

The Farewell

On December 16, 1979, Marshall took the field for the last time as the Vikings played the New England Patriots in Foxboro, Massachusetts. He was playing in his 282nd consecutive regular-season game, 302nd overall including play-off appearances. He had taken part in every game ever played by the Minnesota Vikings since their opener against the Chicago Bears when they entered the National Football League back in 1961.

His Minnesota farewell had taken place the week before when the Vikings hosted the Buffalo Bills in Metropolitan Stadium.

Marshall was honored by his teammates at midfield prior to the game. Less than a month shy of his forty-second birthday, he then went out and sacked Buffalo quarterback Joe Ferguson two times to lead Minnesota to a 10–3 win over the Bills. He was given the game ball by coach Bud Grant and carried off the field by his teammates.

Perhaps the greatest praise of all was bestowed on Marshall later by his former coach. Said the man who coached Fran Tarkenton, Alan Page, and several other Hall of Famers, "Many times people ask coaches who their greatest player was. It's normally very hard to choose, but I don't hesitate to say Jim Marshall."[33]

The Toughest Battle of All

On Sunday, November 28, 1999, the Vikings retired Marshall's uniform number 70 on Jim Marshall Day. His was the fourth Viking player to have his number retired, joining Fran Tarkenton, Paul Krause, and Alan Page. Marshall was recognized for his excellence on the field and for his amazing record for consecutive games played. For Marshall, it was something he wanted—not had—to do. "I never wanted to miss a game," he would say. "It was a thrill for me every time I had an opportunity to go out on the field. I just never wanted to be sitting on the sidelines."[34]

Marshall was sick or injured numerous times during the streak, but never enough to miss a game. "He played better when he was hurt," recalled Grant, "because he focused on not letting the injury get the better of him."[35]

Unfortunately, sickness caught up to Marshall in 2000. In August of that year, he revealed that he was suffering from prostate cancer that had spread to his bones. Marshall faced this setback with a positive attitude. "To me," he said, "this is just a part of life that ultimately we may all expect to have to go through. If you're not prepared for the adversities of life, the battles you may have to fight, you're going to be in real trouble."[36]

It was not long before Marshall had to face another obstacle. On July 6, 2001, he was riding in a car that skidded off a winding road and rolled over several times on its way down the side of a hill. His seat belt probably saved his life, but he still suffered

injuries to his ribs and ver-
tebrae. The injuries, however, were not severe enough
to cause him to miss Jim
Marshall's Inner City Cele-
brity Golf Tournament,
which benefits Life's Missing Link, an organization
he cofounded that works
with troubled youngsters.
To those who know him,
Marshall's appearance was
not a surprise. It was another example of his com-
mitment to a cause in which
he believed.

Marshall's commitment
to the game of football was
never questioned. He re-
tired having played in four
Super Bowls and two Pro
Bowls. He played twenty
seasons in the NFL, nine-
teen of them with Minnesota.

*Marshall addresses the crowd in a 1999
ceremony in which his number was
retired.*

He was cocaptain of the Vikings for seventeen years and played
on eleven division champions. When he retired, his 282 games
played were second on the all-time list behind quarterback-
kicker George Blanda. (In 2001, Tennessee Titans guard Bruce
Matthews played in his 283rd game to eclipse Marshall's mark
for a nonkicker.)

The record for which he will always be remembered, however, is his consecutive game streak. In 1995, *Sports Illustrated*
magazine asked a panel of five longtime football observers to
pick the NFL records most likely to never be broken. All five
agreed that Marshall's streak was at the top of the list. As former NFL coach Hank Stram put it, "We'll see another star in
the east before that happens again."[37]

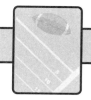

CHAPTER 4

Bud Grant

Bud Grant is unquestionably the greatest coach the Minnesota Vikings have ever had. His teams won eleven division titles, one NFL championship, and three NFC crowns. Although he never won a Super Bowl, his teams reached football's ultimate game on four separate occasions, making him one of the few coaches ever to do so. He retired with 158 NFL wins to his credit.

Overcoming a Handicap

Harry Peter Grant Jr. was born on May 20, 1927, in the shipping town of Superior, Wisconsin. He was the oldest child of Harry Peter Sr. and Bernice Grant. Because his mother did not like the confusion caused by a pair of Harrys, she began calling the youngster Buddy Boy. This eventually was shortened to Bud. The Grants had a daughter after Bud, but she died at birth. Two other sons, Jim and Jack, followed several years later. Because of the age difference, said Bud, "I baby-sat my brothers a lot, but we were never really close."[38]

Bud's father was a fireman who worked hard to provide for his wife and kids. There was always food on the table, but life during the Depression did not allow for many luxuries.

As a child, Bud contracted polio, which would leave him with one leg shorter than the other. Rather than giving him any special treatment to counteract the disease, the family doctor said his best therapy would be a ball and a glove. He encouraged Bud to become as active as possible, with the result that the youngster developed into an all-around athlete. Bud began with baseball, but because of the cold weather in Wisconsin, spent more time playing football and basketball.

By the time Bud was in junior high school, he was organizing games between the neighborhood kids. "We didn't have school teams at that age," he explained, "so I was the one who called kids from another school and made arrangements. I even made out our lineup."[39]

As a fourteen-year-old freshman at Central High School, Bud made the football team as a reserve fullback. He was also a starter on the basketball squad that reached the semifinals of the state tournament. He eventually won conference and regional honors in both sports. In baseball, Bud was a star pitcher who was good enough to be named to *Esquire* magazine's East-West High School All-Star Game, a contest featuring the best high school players in the country.

By the time Bud was a senior, he was being courted by numerous colleges for both basketball and football. With the country involved in World War II, however, school was less of a priority. He enlisted in the navy after graduation and left for the Great Lakes Naval Training Center in July 1945.

The legendary Paul Brown (pictured) coached Bud Grant at the Great Lakes Naval Training Center.

While at Great Lakes, Grant played end under the tutelage of the legendary Paul Brown, who was the squad's coach. He learned more than just football from Brown. "I learned more about people than anything else from Brown," recalled Grant. "He excelled at evaluating people, recognizing what they could and couldn't do. He was able to get the right player into the situation that was right for him."[40] Grant would apply many of the lessons he learned at Great Lakes when he turned to coaching after his playing days were over.

The National Basketball Association

Following his discharge from the service, Grant enrolled at the University of Minnesota. As a freshman, he was a starter on the baseball, football, and basketball teams. When he moved up to the varsity, he won a total of nine letters in the three sports. Many people today still consider him the most versatile athlete in the school's history.

One of the first people Grant met at Minnesota was Sid Hartman, a reporter covering the Gophers for the *Minneapolis Times.* Hartman was also involved in the operation of the Minneapolis Lakers basketball team of the National Basketball Association (NBA). In the winter of Grant's senior year, Hartman told him about a position that had opened up on the team due to an injury. As Grant later explained, "There wasn't really a lot of talk, it just seemed like a good opportunity. By Christmas, I was playing in the NBA."[41]

Grant signed with the Lakers for $3,500. Although not a star, he was a good rebounder and played excellent defense. The Lakers were led by the sport's first great big man, George Mikan. With Grant playing a reserve role at small forward, Minneapolis won the league championship in the 1949–50 season. In describing his role, Grant said, "I wasn't a great basketball player. I played on a great team, and there were times I was able to contribute to our success."[42]

Although Grant was playing professional basketball, he had not been forgotten by the NFL. He was taken by the Philadelphia Eagles as the twelfth overall selection in the 1950 college draft. Philadelphia offered him a contract for $7,500, less than what he thought he was worth. He turned them down and continued to play for the Lakers in 1950–51.

By the end of his second NBA season, however, Grant realized that his future was not in basketball. He contacted the Eagles and joined them in training camp for the 1951 season. At six feet, three inches tall and 200 pounds, Grant played defensive end for Philadelphia and led the squad in quarterback sacks.

The following year, he was offered the same salary he had signed for as a rookie. He refused to sign, but agreed to play. In this way, he would play out his option and become free to sign with someone else in 1953.

Grant switched to offense in 1952 and earned a starting job at end. He caught fifty-seven passes for the year, second in the league and tops on the Eagles. For his performance, he was selected to play in the annual Pro Bowl. The Eagles, however, told him he would not be allowed to go if he did not sign a contract. Grant left the team and joined the Winnipeg Blue Bombers of the Canadian Football League (CFL). He signed with them for $2,000 more than what Philadelphia had offered. In doing so, he became the first NFL player to play out his option and jump to another team in another league.

A Canadian League Hall of Famer

Grant excelled with the Blue Bombers right from the start. Playing offensive end, he caught sixty-eight passes in his first season to lead the team. He also played defensive back and set a CFL record by intercepting five passes in a single game against the Regina Roughriders.

Grant led Winnipeg in receptions in each of his four seasons with the team, and totaled 216 for his career. He also played in the Canadian All-Star Game three times. Following his appearance in the 1956 contest, Grant was called in by Winnipeg management and offered the job of coaching the team. The twenty-nine-year-old accepted the position and began going about the business of improving the squad.

In Grant's very first year in charge, Winnipeg posted a 13-3 record and continued on to the Grey Cup, Canadian football's version of the Super Bowl. It would become a regular occurrence for Grant's teams, who reached the Cup six times, and won on four of those occasions, in his ten years at the helm. His record over that time was 105 wins, 53 losses, and 2 ties.

In Grant's last three years at Winnipeg, he also served as the team's general manager. He found it hard to carry out the duties of both positions at the same time. "The one job can tend to inhibit the other," he said. "As coach, it's your job to convince a player that he's doing a good job. But when you sit down to negotiate a contract with him as general manager, you're coming from a different direction. It's difficult to take a fellow down a peg in negotiations, and then try to build him up out on the field."[43]

Bud Grant signed his first contract as the Vikings head coach in 1966.

The Vikings Come Calling

Since 1961, the expansion Minnesota Vikings franchise of the NFL had been after Grant to leave Winnipeg and come to Minnesota as the new team's head coach. Grant had turned them down, however, insistent on fulfilling his obligations to Winnipeg. By 1966, he began to think about the job more seriously. When it was offered to him again by Vikings' general manager Jim Finks, he accepted. He signed a three-year contract calling for salaries of $32,000, $34,000, and $36,000.

Grant saw his job in Minnesota as one of fine-tuning, rather than rebuilding, the team. "We want to grow," he said. "We want to build on what is already here. But we aren't rebuilding. . . . The foundation of this team is already in place."[44] The key characteristic he wanted to instill in the club was discipline. He managed every minute detail, including how the players stood during the playing of the national anthem before the game.

Grant's theories on coaching centered on discipline. In order to develop this in his players, one of the things he did was make the team practice in the cold weather. He also refused to allow heaters on the sideline during games. In this way, he reasoned, the players learned that the cold would always be a factor and that winning was the only thing that would make it bearable.

Grant also knew it was imperative that the club get a quarterback who could help it learn how to win. The player he had in mind for the position was a scrappy CFL quarterback by the name of Joe Kapp. Finks was able to sign him for Grant's first year of 1967. As Grant later recalled, "He became the image of the Vikings. . . . He was a competitor. He'd battle anybody. That quality, his toughness, drew players to him."[45]

The Vikings began the 1967 season by losing their first four games. Grant's first NFL win came in game 5. It was a particularly satisfying one, coming as it did in his native Wisconsin against the defending NFL champion Green Bay Packers. Still, Minnesota finished the year in last place in the Central Division with a record of three wins, eight losses, and three ties. There were indications of good things for the future, however, as four of the eight losses were by six points or less.

The next year, with Kapp showing the way, the Vikings started to turn things around. The team added several key players, including offensive tackle Ron Yary and safety Paul Krause. Minnesota finished at 8–6 and made the play-offs for the first time in franchise history. Grant knew the team was headed in the right direction.

Super Bowl IV

The Vikings began 1969 on a negative note, losing the season opener to the New York Giants (and former Minnesota quarterback Fran Tarkenton) by a score of 24–23. They also lost their final regular-season game to the Atlanta Falcons. In between, however, they reeled off a string of twelve consecutive wins to give them the NFL Central Division title.

The Vikings defense (in white) rushes the Kansas City Chiefs' kicker (3) in the 1970 Super Bowl.

In compiling their 12–2 mark, the Viking defense—led by the Purple People Eaters—allowed only 133 points, a record for the modern era. The club moved on to the play-offs where they defeated the Los Angeles Rams (23–20) and the Cleveland Browns (27–7). The wins put them in Super Bowl IV as two-touchdown favorites over the Kansas City Chiefs, champions of the American Football League. The game would be the last ever played by an AFL team, as the circuit's ten clubs would become members of the newly formed American Football Conference of the NFL the next season.

The Chiefs surprised the Vikings and most NFL observers. Playing in front of almost eighty-one thousand fans in Tulane Stadium, Kansas City took a 16–0 lead into the locker room at halftime. Minnesota managed to score a touchdown in the third quarter, but it was matched by the Chiefs who came out on top by a score of 23–7.

Prior to the 1970 season, Kapp left Minnesota to sign with the New England Patriots as a free agent. Minnesota continued its winning ways without missing a beat. Grant guided the club into the play-offs again in 1970 and 1971, but the Vikings were eliminated in the first round both years.

The following season, the Vikings reacquired quarterback Tarkenton in a trade with the Giants and looked forward to a return to the top. Unfortunately, the season turned into a disappointment. The team struggled to a .500 record (8–8), and Grant let it be known he would not accept similar results the next year. "You'd better take a look at yourselves and see if you intend to play football next year," he told the players in the dressing room after the final game, "because this isn't going to happen again."[46]

Domination and Disappointment

Grant proved to be true to his word. Fullback Chuck Foreman was drafted out of the University of Miami in the first round of

Coach Grant relays a play through a headset in 1972, the year the Vikings reacquired quarterback Fran Tarkenton (far right).

the 1973 college draft and anchored the Minnesota running game. Over the next six seasons (1973 through 1978), Minnesota won six NFC Central Division titles and compiled an overall record of 62–22–2. The Vikings won conference championships in 1973, 1974, and 1976, earning themselves three more trips to the Super Bowl. Unfortunately for Grant, they would fall short of winning a ring each time.

In Super Bowl VIII, Minnesota was defeated by the Miami Dolphins, 24–7. The Vikings' lone touchdown came in the final quarter after Miami had already scored all of its points.

The following year, the Vikings were matched up against the Pittsburgh Steelers, who were playing for the NFL championship for the first time in their forty-two-year history. The battle between the two clubs was dominated by the defenses. Led by quarterback Terry Bradshaw, the Steelers scored a pair of touchdowns in the second half to seal a 16–6 victory. Some people blamed Minnesota's sluggish performance on the team's week of inactivity before the game. Grant, however, refused to make excuses, instead attributing the loss to the Vikings' failure to come up with big plays when they were needed.

Two years later, Grant's forces met the Oakland Raiders in Super Bowl XI. The Vikings could not stop the punishing Oakland attack. For the fourth time in four Super Bowls, they failed to score in the first half. By that time, the Raiders had already jumped out to a sixteen-point lead. They matched that total in the second half and came away with a 32–14 win. As Tarkenton said after the game, "They totally dominated us. We have no excuses."[47] For the fourth time in eight years, the Vikings had come up short in their bid to win a championship.

An Enviable Record

The year 1976 marked an end to a remarkable stretch of seven years out of eight in which Minnesota won ten or more games during the regular season. The Vikings continued to be competitive, but a championship still evaded them. Grant remained as head coach until the mid-1980s. Following the team's 8–8 mark in 1983, he announced his retirement after seventeen years at the helm in Minnesota. "I decided this was the time to quit," he said. "There wasn't any pressure on me. There are a lot of things I want to do while I still have my health."[48]

Grant led the Vikings to 158 victories during his tenure as head coach.

quit," he said. "There wasn't any pressure on me. There are a lot of things I want to do while I still have my health."[48]

Grant remained with the team in 1984 as a consultant while Les Steckel took over on the field. When the Vikings struggled through a disastrous 3–13 season, however, Grant returned as head coach. After guiding Minnesota to a 7–9 mark in 1985, he retired for good, turning over the reins to assistant coach Jerry Burns.

Grant's career NFL ledger as Minnesota's head coach shows 158 wins, 96 losses, and 5 ties. His teams made it to the play-offs twelve times, winning 10 games and losing 12. He led the Vikings with a calm, confident demeanor that served a clear purpose. As he explained, "Players take their cue from the coaches. If the coaches don't have enthusiasm or are not optimistic, the players will pick up on that attitude. You have to be realistic, but you can't get down."[49]

As a coach, Grant prepared his players to the best of his ability, then let them play the game. He was smart enough to realize there were some things beyond his control. "There are coaches who spend 18 hours a day coaching the perfect game," he once said, "and they lose because the ball is oval and they can't control the bounce."[50] In recognition of his record over eighteen seasons, Grant was elected to the Pro Football Hall of Fame in 1994.

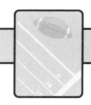

CHAPTER 5

Alan Page

A lan Page was a fixture on the Minnesota Vikings defensive line for twelve seasons. A perennial All-Pro, he was the NFL's Most Valuable Player in 1971, the only time a defensive player has been so honored. He gained distinction as the game's first outstanding pass-rushing defensive tackle, whose exceptional quickness and pursuit enabled him to get into opposing backfields with regularity. When his playing career ended, he served in the Minnesota attorney general's office and later became an associate justice for the Minnesota Supreme Court.

Strong Values

Alan Cedric Page was one of four children born to Georgianna Umbles and Howard Felix Page. He was born in Canton, Ohio—the future home of the Pro Football Hall of Fame—on August 7, 1945. In a town where many of the adults worked in the steel mills, Alan's mother was a country club attendant and his father a bar manager. They instilled strong values and a love of learning in Alan, his brother Howard, and his sisters Marvel and Twila. "I grew up in a family where education was valued," Page told *Parade* magazine in 1994. "It was made clear to me by my parents that if I was going to be successful, if I was going to have a better life than they had, then I was going to have to perform in the classroom."[51]

Unlike many other youngsters, Alan did not dream of becoming a professional athlete. "Football was something I happened to do," he said. "In my mind's eye, I never saw myself as a football player—not even when I was a little kid growing up in Canton, Ohio."[52] He did not take up the sport until the ninth grade, and then only because his older brother did.

Instead, Alan imagined himself as an attorney. "Long before I had an interest in football," he recalled, "I had an interest in law. My earliest recollections are from fourth grade, back when you don't have any idea what the law is about. It was probably a little to do with Perry Mason, but also a sense, without knowing any lawyers, that, viewed from the 11-year-old's eyes, the law is an easy life, you make lots of money, you play golf every afternoon. That looked a lot more interesting than the steel mill."[53]

Alan attended Central Catholic High School in Canton. He tried out for the football team and was an immediate sensation. He starred as a defensive lineman, where one opposing coach called him "the best high school player I ever saw."[54] Over the course of his years at Central, he made the All-City, All-County, and All-State teams. As a senior in 1962, he was recruited by many colleges. He eventually accepted a scholarship to the University of Notre Dame in South Bend, Indiana.

Page starred for three years as a defensive end with the Fighting Irish. He was a member of their 1966 National Championship squad and won All-American honors as a senior. He graduated in 1967 with a bachelor's degree in political science. That spring, he was selected by the Minnesota Vikings as their third pick in the first round (number fifteen overall) of the NFL draft.

Welcome to the NFL

Right from the beginning, Page showed that he was his own man, with his own set of values and principles. During training camp of his rookie year, the veteran players on the team had a tradition of taking the rookies out and getting them so drunk that they got sick. "I don't drink beer," Page told *Sports History*

Alan Page was Minnesota's third pick of the 1967 NFL draft.

magazine. "I never have. I just don't like the taste. So I told them I wasn't going to drink. That was a problem because here was this guy who thought he was too good to do what all the rookies are supposed to do."[55]

Eventually, however, things worked out. "The next day at practice was not the most pleasant experience I ever had," continued Page. "But I didn't get rejected, either. There seemed to be a sense on the part of the other players that I was a little different and I wasn't going to conform. I think some of them respected me for that."[56]

Minnesota coach Bud Grant never started rookies, preferring to let them learn by watching the veterans. Page's outstanding play during training camp and the exhibition season, however, made him change his mind. Page stepped right into the Vikings' starting lineup at defensive tackle, despite the fact that he had played defensive end at Notre Dame. He made his presence felt in his very first year, recovering three fumbles and anchoring the front four of the Vikings' Purple People Eaters defense. (Page personally hated the nickname. "I am not purple," he said, "and I don't eat people."[57])

At six feet, four inches tall and 245 pounds, Page was somewhat small for the position. He more than made up for it with his quickness, however. He was so quick, he would occasionally reach the runner before the handoff was even made. Unlike other defensive tackles, Page did not wear arm pads while he played. He believed he could get around blockers with his quickness rather than have to hit them and push them aside.

Page motions toward a runner from the opposing team. Unlike other defensive tackles, Page relied on speed, not brute force, to get past blockers.

A Dominating Defender

Minnesota won just three games in 1967, but over the next few years, they developed one of the most dominating defenses in pro football, with Page as its centerpiece. The squad helped the Vikings become the dominant team in the NFC Central Division. From 1968 to 1978, they won their division ten times.

Perhaps Page's greatest attribute as a player was his ability to focus on the ball and not be distracted by other things. As Minnesota defensive line coach Jack Patera said, "Where the ball goes, Alan goes. It doesn't matter if it's a 60-yard pass, he turns and chases it down. That's how he recovers fumbles way down field. That kind of pursuit is something you try to instill in a player. But you can only improve a player's pursuit, you can't teach anyone to do it the way Alan does. It's in you or it isn't."[58]

In 1970, Page was focused enough to recover seven fumbles (converting one into a touchdown) and also make an interception. The following year, he led the Vikings to the NFC Central Division title with an 11–3 mark. He made league history by becoming the first defensive player ever named the league's Most Valuable Player. "I have never seen a player have a year like he did," said Kansas City Chiefs Hall of Famer Buck Buchanan. "He was annihilating people. It was the kind of season you dream about as a player."[59] Page, however, was less impressed. "I don't know whether 1971 was any better than the years before that or the years after," he told *Sports Illustrated.* "But it happens to be when I got the recognition."[60]

Following his MVP season, Page was left with a feeling that there was more that he wanted to do with his life than just play football. "It was like getting to the top of the mountain," he said, "and wondering why you went through all the work to get there. As time has gone on, I've come to understand that climbing the mountain, not getting to the top, was what it was all about. But at this time there was this real sense that there must be more to life than this."[61]

Despite these doubts, Page continued to perform at an All-Pro level. In 1976, he recorded twenty-one and a-half sacks, an amazing total for a defensive tackle. After racing through the regular season with an 11–2–1 record, the Vikings defeated the

Redskins and Rams to move into the Super Bowl against the Oakland Raiders. Although they were chosen by many to win in their fourth appearance in football's biggest game, the Vikings again fell short of a championship by losing, 32–14. In the locker room after the game, Page outraged many Minnesota fans by refusing to treat the loss as a matter of life and death. "How on earth can otherwise sensible people get so involved in a football game?" he asked. "You could measure the lasting impact on the lives of the people who played in it and those who watched it at just about zero."[62] The words were not meant to express a lack of feeling, but simply showed that Page understood that life still went on despite the loss.

On to Chicago

By 1978, Page began to think even more seriously about life after football. He took up running to help keep himself in shape. As he explained, "I didn't want to turn into a tub of lard when my playing days were over."[63] The running, however, had an unexpected side effect.

Because of his strenuous training regimen, Page's weight dropped from a high of 245 down to 220. Minnesota coach Grant did not approve of the change, believing he was too light to play his position well. He spoke to Page about the situation, but could not get his All-Pro tackle to change his ways. "I talked to Alan about his running," said Grant, "but he remained firm in his position. We have offered him to other teams, but no one has shown any interest."[64] Despite the fact that his performance had not dropped significantly, the Vikings placed him on waivers. He was claimed by the Chicago Bears and joined them midway through the 1978 season.

Page picked up right where he had left off in Minnesota. Despite missing six of the Bears' games, he still led Chicago with eleven and a-half sacks. He also recorded sixty tackles to rank second among the team's defensive linemen. The next season, he again topped the team in sacks while leading Chicago to a 10–6 record and the wild card spot in the play-offs.

By this time, age was beginning to catch up with the veteran. Page played his final NFL game on December 20, 1981. The Bears defeated the Denver Broncos that day, 35–24, in the chilly

In 1978 Page led the Bears with eleven and a half sacks and sixty tackles.

twelve degree temperatures of Soldier Field in Chicago. At the age of thirty-six, Page sacked Denver quarterback Craig Morton three and a half times in his farewell performance. In his three and a half years with the Bears, he totaled forty sacks and twelve blocked kicks.

Another remarkable achievement was Page's record as an iron man. He never missed a game in his NFL career, a streak that included 218 regular season games, 16 play-off games, and 4 Super Bowls. The mark is a reflection of the strong work ethic instilled in him by his parents.

Welcome to the Hall of Fame

On July 30, 1988, Page was enshrined in the Pro Football Hall of Fame. He became the first hometown native to be elected to the shrine. (Cleveland Browns fullback Marion Motley played high school ball in Canton, but was born in Georgia.)

When a player is inducted into the Hall, he selects someone as his presenter to make an introductory speech. That person is generally a former coach or teammate. In Page's case, he chose Willarene Beasley, the principal of North High School in Minneapolis. He selected her because she was a black educator, representative of minorities. In the Hall's twenty-five-year existence, she was the first presenter without any football connection. Her speech focused more on Page's belief in education than on his feats on the football field.

Page's acceptance speech was also unusual. "On this occasion," he said, "I ask myself, 'What contribution can I still make that would be truly worthy of the outpouring of respect and good feelings as I have felt here today?' And the answer, for me, is clear: 'To help give other children the chance to reach their dreams.'"[65] He established the nonprofit Page Education Foundation to provide scholarships to local high school students. Since the foundation's inception, more than eleven hundred students have been helped. In return, the recipients are required to return to their communities to act as tutors and mentors for elementary school children. For his work in encouraging minority students to stick with their education, Page was awarded the 1991 Friend of Education Award by the National Education Association.

A Career in Law

Back during the 1974 season, Page had been in the league for eight years. Knowing he would not be able to play football forever, he began preparing for his postfootball career by enrolling in the University of Minnesota law school. He took courses all year round and completed his degree requirements in 1978. He passed the bar examination in 1979 on his second attempt while he was still an active player. "Thurgood Marshall, Roy Wilkins, and Martin Luther King Jr., were individuals who helped develop my interest in the law," he recalled. "They sparked my interest because of their beliefs and actions in seeking equal justice and equal opportunity."[66]

After retiring, Page went to work for the Minneapolis-based law firm of Lindquist & Vennum, which served as counsel to the NFL Players Association. He moved his practice into the Minnesota attorney general's office in 1985, specializing in issues of employment litigation. Two years later, he was appointed assistant attorney general. Six years after that, he was elected as the first African-American associate justice on the Minnesota Supreme Court.

Since his retirement, Page has devoted more time to his running. "I run between 50 and 60 miles a week during good weather," he said, "and I try to get out every day." [67] In addition to being the first NFL player to finish a full 26.2 mile marathon (in

---

As a Minnesota Supreme Court Associate Justice, Alan Page addresses a question during a 2001 press conference.

1979), he has also completed the sixty-two-mile Edmund Fitzgerald Ultra-Marathon along Minnesota's Lake Superior shore.

Putting Everything in Perspective

Page posted impressive statistics over the course of his fifteen seasons in the NFL. In addition to his Most Valuable Player award in 1971 and his four NFC Defensive Player of the Year trophies (1971, 1973, 1974, and 1975), he was also named All-Pro nine consecutive times. He totaled 173 quarterback sacks in his career, or about 12 a season. By unofficial records, he also blocked 28 punts or kicks, recovered 23 fumbles, and batted down 41 passes. Page's success was all the more remarkable considering that to him, football was not a matter of life and death. "You'd think you'd have to love what you're doing to play in the fashion that I have," he said. "But I don't love it. I've just always done the best I could."[68]

Page has been able to keep things in perspective and put football in its proper place. "Football's just entertainment," he said. "Its importance in the world is blown out of proportion to what it really is."[69] To Page, the things that matter most are people, particularly children. As he has said, "If I could choose a way to be remembered, it wouldn't be my association with football. Football is the past—a good past, but I'd want to be remembered with children—my children and other children."[70]

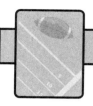

CHAPTER 6

Cris Carter

Cris Carter retired in May 2002 as one of the most prolific receivers in NFL history. He stands second on the league's all-time list in receptions and touchdown receptions. He made eight Pro Bowl appearances in his fifteen years in the league and was a model of consistency, with eight one thousand-yard seasons to his credit. He was also honored with the first Walter Payton NFL Man of the Year Award for his charitable works off the field of play.

Growing Up in the Midwest

Christopher D. Carter was born on November 25, 1965, in Troy, Ohio, a town of approximately twenty thousand located in the western part of the state. He was the sixth of seven children born to Clarence and Joyce Carter. Cris's oldest brother, Butch, served as a father figure for the other kids, since their real father was seldom around. Clarence and Joyce eventually divorced when Cris was still a toddler.

A short time later, Joyce moved the family south to Middletown, Ohio, a middle-class steel town. There, she took a new job to support her brood. Although their neighborhood was rough and her family was poor, Joyce tried to instill her children with good Christian values.

Cris was involved in sports from a very early age. Since his brother Butch was an All-American basketball player, it was only natural that basketball was Cris's first love. By age seven, he already knew that he would be a professional athlete when he grew up. Even at that age, he always wanted to do his best, and would not accept anyone else who did less. He demonstrated his competitive fire in his very first peewee football game when he was eight. When his young teammates went after an opposing player halfheartedly, Cris began screaming at them. Butch had to finally drag him off the field. (Butch always watched out for his little brother. As their mother once explained, "Butch paved the way for Cris. Every mistake that Butch made in his career, he made sure that his brother didn't."[71])

One of the people who had a strong influence on Cris was George Kinnerly, his basketball coach in junior high school. Kinnerly once kicked him off the team and made him miss a game because of misconduct. It made Cris realize how much he loved the sport and helped him develop a better work ethic. He learned it was important to play by the rules and

Cris Carter's older brother Butch (12) gets schooled by the Lakers' Magic Johnson in a 1984 game.

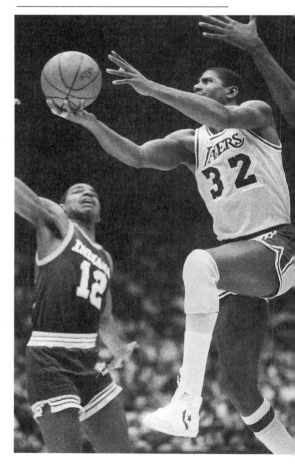

imperative that he listen to his coach if he wanted to play. Coach Kinnerly also helped him understand the importance of keeping up with his schoolwork. As Carter wrote in his 2000 book, *Born to Believe*, "I understood that he believed in me and he spent a lot of time with me to make sure I was conscientious."[72]

Basketball or Football?

Although Cris's first love was basketball, he also enjoyed football. At Middletown High School, he starred at end on coach Bill Conley's team. Conley convinced him that if he worked hard, he could become an All-American. Cris believed him and had an excellent junior year, making the All-Ohio team as a split end. The next season, he closed out his high school career by catching eighty passes for over two thousand yards. He was a *Parade* magazine All-American that year (1983), fulfilling his coach's prophecy. By the time he graduated, he was the school's all-time leader in both receptions and touchdowns.

Cris was still heavily involved in basketball, however. He scored over sixteen hundred points in his high school career and was recruited by a number of colleges in both sports. He narrowed his choices down to the University of Louisville for basketball, and Ohio State University for football. After consulting with his coaches, he finally decided to accept a football scholarship to OSU.

Difficulties at OSU

Like many young people in his neighborhood in Middletown, Carter was tempted by alcohol and drugs. He began drinking and experimenting with drugs at age fifteen because of peer pressure, but continued using them because they made him feel good. When he enrolled at Ohio State in 1984, his addictions continued, although the drug testing athletes had to submit to made him limit his usage.

Carter's substance abuse did not seem to affect his performance on the field. In his freshman year, he set a Rose Bowl record with 172 receiving yards in OSU's 20–17 loss to the University of Southern California. By the end of his third year, he had already been chosen to the All–Big Ten team twice. He made All-American in his junior year and already was the school's all-time leader in receptions (168) and touchdown catches (27).

On April 23, 1987, however, Carter's college career received a serious setback when he was suspended for rules violations. Three months later, he was declared ineligible for his senior season for having accepted money and signed a contract with sports agents Lloyd Bloom and Norby Walters to have them represent him in any future negotiations. Carter was just one of many college athletes caught up in the widespread scandal.

The probe of the two agents eventually led to Carter being indicted on charges of mail fraud and obstruction of justice. He pleaded guilty to having defrauded the school and concealing the money he received. He was sentenced to perform six hundred hours of community service work and was fined $15,000.

OSU receiver Cris Carter (2) makes a flying catch in the 1985 Citrus Bowl.

While this was happening, the NFL decided to hold a supplemental draft to select players who had been involved in the scandal. Carter was selected by the Philadelphia Eagles in the fourth round of that 1987 draft.

The Low Point

Carter's first taste of NFL action left much to be desired. He caught his first NFL pass in Philadelphia's fifth game of the 1987 season. It was a twenty-two-yarder good for a touchdown. Unfortunately, he caught only four other passes that year in a disappointing debut.

Carter experienced more success over the next two seasons. In 1988, he averaged 19.5 yards per catch, and the next year he led the team with eleven touchdown receptions. Overall, however, his play was less than what the Eagles expected. Coach Buddy Ryan, annoyed by what he considered Carter's poor work ethic and concerned about his chemical dependency, put him on waivers prior to the start of the 1990 season. "All he can do," said Ryan sarcastically, "is catch passes in the end zone."[73] On waivers, any team could claim Carter for just one hundred dollars. The Minnesota Vikings immediately did so.

Turning It Around

Being released by the Eagles was the lowest point, emotionally, in Carter's life. "I was demoralized," he said. "I had started to believe what people were saying about me fading and becoming washed up so young. I was fumbling my way through a life filled with pain, expectations and temptation. I had lost sight of myself and what made me happy, and was far from being content."[74]

Carter began to look more carefully at his life. He admitted his dependency, and with the encouragement of his wife began to get his career and life in order. "When I went to Minnesota," he later said, "I was a young kid, when I left, I was a full-grown man. I gained my sobriety there. There are so many things about Minnesota I will never forget. I will always be indebted to the people of Minnesota."[75]

In Carter's first year at Minnesota, he played behind Anthony Carter and Hassan Jones. He caught 27 passes for the year, including a 78-yarder that was the team's longest play of the season. The next year, he led the team in receptions with 72 and receiving yards with 962.

Prior to the 1992 season, the Vikings acquired All-Pro running back Roger Craig from the San Francisco 49ers for whom he had played on three Super Bowl championship teams. When Carter asked him the secret of his success, he replied, "We take our off-seasons seriously."[76] From that point on, Carter began to work more strenuously at keeping himself in top shape between seasons.

The All-Pro Receiver

Carter's pro career took off in 1993. He set a then–career high in both receptions (86) and receiving yards (1,071) and earned his first trip to the Pro Bowl. The next year he set a league record (since broken) by catching an amazing 122 passes. Fourteen of those passes (for 167 yards) came in a single game against the Arizona Cardinals. Carter was rewarded for his season with his second Pro Bowl selection and first as a starter.

Carter's growth as a player coincided with his growth as a person. He became more of a spiritual person and got involved in a variety of causes. In September 1994, he received the NFL Extra Effort Award for outstanding commitment to community service activities.

Over the next several years, Carter established himself as one of the top receivers

Carter (right) clenches the ball in anticipation of a tackle by the oncoming Tampa Bay defender.

in NFL history. With his size (six feet, three inches tall and 195 pounds) and aggressiveness, he was always on the attack after catching the ball, lunging forward when tackled to get every last inch possible. In 1995, Carter caught 122 balls for the second consecutive year, setting an NFL record for most catches in a two-year span. His seventeen touchdown receptions tied for the league lead and set a new single-season Vikings mark. He also set a team record for receiving yards with 1,371. Over a four-week stretch from November to December, he became the first player in league history to have two or more touchdown catches in four consecutive games.

Carter followed up with ninety-six catches in 1996 to lead the Vikings for a record sixth straight season. The next year, he teamed with Jake Reed to become the first wide-receiving duo to surpass the one thousand-receiving-yards mark four years in a row. Carter also set team records for consecutive games with a touchdown reception (six) and most one hundred-yard receiving games in a career (twenty-three). To show their appreciation for his efforts, the Vikings rewarded Carter with a four-year contract extension worth $23.5 million, making him the highest-paid wide receiver in the league.

By this time, Carter was one of the team's acknowledged leaders. He became an ordained minister in the off-season and tried to set an example for other players to follow. He did not hesitate to get after players or officials who he thought were giving less than their best effort. His style occasionally was questioned by some of his teammates, but they never questioned his leadership. "There are a dozen ways to define a leader," said one veteran player. "Carter gives you most of them. You've got to agree he's a one-in-a-thousand football player."[77]

An All-Time Great

In 1998, Carter set a new Minnesota team record with his seventy-seventh touchdown. The old mark had been held by fullback Bill Brown. Carter averaged 13.0 yards per catch for the second-highest mark of his career. He teamed up with rookie Randy Moss to form the league's most devastating pass-catching duo.

A year later, Carter led the NFL with thirteen touchdown receptions. Included were a team-record seven consecutive games with a touchdown catch. When Minnesota played the Tampa Bay Buccaneers in early December 1999, he went past the ten thousand-yard receiving mark for his Vikings' career. Carter also set personal postseason highs with seven catches for 111 yards against the Rams in the divisional play-off game. Despite his success, however, the Vikings lost to the eventual Super Bowl champion Rams.

Following the season, Carter was named as the first recipient of the Walter Payton NFL Man of the Year Award for his work with inner-city children and other community activities. Unlike some other athletes, Carter welcomed the chance to be a role model for young people.

Carter celebrates after completing a four-yard touchdown against the San Diego Chargers in November 1999.

"We can make an impact," he said. "We can make a difference in people's lives. It's time to stand up, make our stand that we can be different and make good choices."[78]

Carter followed up his 1999 season with another excellent year in 2000. He led the Vikings in receptions for the tenth straight season with ninety-six while recording the second-highest yardage total of his career (1,274). On November 30, he caught the one-thousandth pass of his career, becoming only the second person in NFL history to reach that milestone. Carter also set a personal single-game record with 168 receiving yards against the Miami Dolphins in September. In January, he had the best postseason performance of his career with eight catches for 120 yards against the New Orleans Saints in the divisional play-off. He did not know it at the time, but it was the next to last play-off appearance of his career.

A Miscalculation

Following the win over the Saints, the Vikings were defeated by the New York Giants in the NFC championship game, 41–0. Once again, Carter came up short in his quest for a trip to the Super Bowl. When running back Robert Smith retired, prospects for the future were not looking bright.

Prior to the 2001 season, the Vikings suffered a tragic loss when tackle Korey Stringer died of heatstroke during training camp. The team never seemed to recover from the blow, compiling a 5–11 record and finishing ahead of only Detroit in the NFC Central Division.

Carter's performance was affected as much as anyone's. He caught just seventy-three passes for his lowest total since 1992. He also alienated many fans with his antics on the sidelines, which included yelling at defensive players and arguing with coaches. At age thirty-six, Carter knew he did not have many years left to play, with his dream of a Super Bowl ring looking less and less likely. After hinting at retirement, he decided to exercise his option to get out of the remaining year of his contract and test free agency.

The powerful St. Louis Rams expressed interest in signing Carter in what appeared to be a perfect fit for him. He was set to meet with Rams coach Mike Martz, but at the last minute, Carter decided to delay his appointment in order to travel to Cleveland to talk to the Browns. The Rams refused to reschedule and when the Browns offer fell through, Carter was left without a team. "I shouldn't have gone to Cleveland," he later said. "And if I did, I should have gone there later in the recruiting process."[79]

Instead of accepting a lesser offer from the Miami Dolphins, Carter decided to retire. As he explained, "There is nothing I haven't been able to accomplish, given the circumstances of the teams I've been affiliated with. My career has exceeded my expectations. It'd be nice to say, 'Yes, I won a championship.' But no, I don't feel that because I didn't win a championship that I wasn't successful."[80]

Carter's 2000 season saw him make ninety-six receptions for a total of 1,274 yards.

Television Beckons

Carter retired in 2002 with 1,093 career receptions and 129 touchdown catches. Both marks are second to only Jerry Rice in NFL annals. His 13,833 receiving yards rank him third all-time to Rice and James Lofton. Carter had eight straight seasons with 1,000 or more yards receiving and made eight consecutive trips to the Pro Bowl. When he becomes eligible, it is likely that he will be elected to the Pro Football Hall of Fame on his first try.

Until then, he will take his talents to the television booth. At the same teleconference at which he declared his retirement, he also announced he would be joining the HBO Sports *Inside the NFL* team. As HBO sports president Ross Greenburg said, "Adding Cris puts together one of the more dynamic and really powerful groups of announcers in television."[81] Carter himself was philosophical about the move. "As an athlete," he said, "you'll always have a feeling to play. That will never leave. HBO is not replacing the NFL for me, it's just another phase of my life. . . . I would love to play but I had to make a decision."[82] If Carter brings the same intensity and desire to the television booth as he did to the football field, success in his new career is all but assured.

CHAPTER 7

Randy Moss

In 2001, the *Sporting News* named Randy Moss as the best player in the NFL. He is without question the most explosive receiver playing today, capable of breaking open a game with a single catch. His rare combination of speed, leaping ability, and body control make him impossible to cover in man-to-man situations. His attitude, however, is often questioned, and his work ethic leaves much to be desired. At times it seems as if the only person capable of stopping Moss is Moss himself.

A Childhood Dream

Randy Moss was born on February 13, 1977, in Rand, West Virginia, to Maxine Moss and Randy Pratt. He grew up in the small mining town with his sister, Latisia, and his half brother Eric. Rand is a small community of a few hundred homes located in the Kanawha Valley about fifteen miles south of Charleston. (Kanawha County was famous as the home of basketball legend Jerry West.) Since Rand is unincorporated, technically it is not really a town, and does not even have its own school.

Randy received a strict upbringing from his mother, who was a single parent. She made him attend church regularly and was determined to raise him to become a responsible, caring adult. He generally stayed out of trouble, since most of his free time was spent playing sports. Randy tried to emulate his older half brother, who was an excellent student in school and a star in both basketball and football. Randy's interest in football was kindled when he helped carry equipment for

Randy Moss's speed and agility have earned him a reputation as one of the best players in the NFL.

his brother's midget league team. He developed a love for the game and began dreaming of some day playing in the NFL.

Randy and his brother attended school in nearby Belle, a mostly white community. There, Randy followed Eric at DuPont High School, where the older youngster was an All-State basketball player and an All-American in football.

Most of the blacks at DuPont (approximately 40 of the 670 or so students) kept to themselves, rarely mingling with the white students. They often were the object of racial slurs, particularly so in an area of the school known as Redneck Alley, where Confederate flags and Ku Klux Klan symbols were common sights on lockers. "It's a bad place," remembers Moss. "No kid should have to go to school and hear racial slurs. No one should have to come to school with fear in their heart. Nobody ever really bothered me. But it happened to my friends."[83]

As a standout athlete, Randy drew more than his share of attention. With above-average size, blazing speed, and great leaping ability, he soon was recognized as an outstanding baseball, basketball, and football player. He also starred in track, where he was the state champ in the one hundred and two hundred meters as a sophomore.

In basketball, Moss was named West Virginia's Player of the Year in both his junior and senior seasons. He won the same honor in football in his senior year when he caught thirty-nine passes for 808 yards as a wide receiver, returned three kickoffs for touchdowns, and made seventy-three tackles as a defensive back. He was recruited in football by many colleges, but the choice for him was an easy one. He accepted a scholarship to play at Notre Dame, a school for which he had dreamed of playing since he was twelve years old. Lou Holtz, coach of the Fighting Irish, called Moss one of the best high school football players he had ever seen.

One day early that spring, however, an incident occurred that had a dramatic effect on his future.

The Fight

On March 24, 1995, a black youth at DuPont challenged a white boy to a fight after school following a confrontation involving a racial remark. The black teen, fearing for his safety, asked the six-foot, four-inch, two hundred-pound Moss to accompany him. According to witnesses, the black youth knocked the other boy to the ground and was administering a beating. Moss apparently moved in to pull his friend away, but not before delivering two kicks of his own because "that racial stuff aggravates me."[84]

The white boy suffered a ruptured spleen that put him in the hospital. Moss, who had recently turned eighteen, was arrested, charged with "malicious wounding," and sentenced to thirty days in jail. His friend was not charged, since he was a juvenile. The incident was a big story in the local newspapers. "It was a huge controversy because of who he was," said *Charleston Daily Mail* sports columnist Chuck Landon. "If he had been Randy 'Jones,' there would have been no to-do. But because he was the best athlete in the state, maybe the best ever from West Virginia, it became a *cause celebre.*"[85]

Moss was expelled from DuPont, but eventually got his degree from Cabell Alternative School. In the meantime, however, Notre Dame refused him admission, claiming his application had been improperly filled out. Although Moss admitted that it was filed a month late, he—along with most observers—believed it was turned down because of the fight.

More Trouble

Following the denial of Moss's application, coach Holtz recommended him to Florida State football coach Bobby Bowden. "He was as good as Deion Sanders," recalled Bowden. "Deion's my measuring stick for athletic ability, and this kid was just a bigger Deion."[86] Moss was accepted by Florida State on the condition that he sit out a year until his sentence was completed. (When he was sentenced in August, the judge agreed to let him serve the time over the summer so that he could attend classes.) While finishing out his time, however, he failed a drug test, testing positive for marijuana. His probation was revoked, ninety days of jail time was added to his sentence, and his scholarship to Florida State was canceled.

With a second indiscretion on his record, Moss's college possibilities were severely limited. No Division I team wanted to take a chance on him. As a last resort, he contacted Bob Pruett, a former assistant coach at Florida State and now the head football coach at Marshall University. Pruett accepted him at the Division I-AA school in West Virginia, and Moss joined the Thundering Herd in 1996.

A College Sensation

Moss made the most of this final chance. He scored three touchdowns in his first game and finished the year with nineteen scores. No college receiver in history had ever scored as many touchdowns in his freshman season.

In the Division I-AA play-offs, Moss led Marshall all the way to the championship. His twenty-eight touchdowns for the year tied a record set by all-time great Jerry Rice. His 1,074 receiving yards set another NCAA freshman mark. In addition, Moss led the nation in kickoff returns with an average of thirty-four yards per return.

The following year, Marshall was promoted to the ranks of Division I schools. The move brought out the best in Moss, who continued to shine against the tougher competition. He led Marshall to the Mid-America Conference championship, setting conference records for both receiving yards and touch-down catches in the process. His twenty-five scores set a new Division I record. Moss was named as the winner of the Fred Biletnikoff Award, given annually to the nation's leading receiver. He also finished fourth in the voting for the Heisman Trophy, given to the top college player of the year. After being

Moss takes the podium at the 1997 Heisman Trophy presentation. Moss finished fourth in the voting for the award.

Moss (right) pushes past a West Virginia University defender during a 1997 game. Moss led Marshall University to the Mid-America Conference championship that same year.

named to the All-American team for the second time in two seasons, Moss was ready to take his game to the next level.

Draft Day Disappointment

When draft day 1998 finally arrived, Moss believed he would be one of the first players chosen. Two other episodes, however, made him less attractive to NFL scouts. In the fall of 1997, he and his girlfriend were involved in a domestic dispute that spilled over into the street. "She just ticked me off," said Moss, "and it got out of hand. The only thing I regret was I put my hands on her. . . . I still love her. I didn't want nothing like that to happen. But that's life, I guess."[87] Although no one was injured and neither party wanted to file a complaint, both Moss and his girlfriend were arrested on misdemeanor charges of domestic battery.

The other incident was Moss's failure to attend the NFL combine prior to the college draft. The best college players come to the combine, where they have a chance to showcase their talents and be measured in terms of strength, speed, agility, and so on. Some interpreted Moss's failure to appear as an indication of a negative attitude, while others thought he was afraid of taking a drug test. "You create suspicions," is the way New Orleans Saints coach Mike Ditka put it.[88] In reality, Moss had just undergone complicated oral surgery to have six teeth removed and was in no condition to perform.

Because of this combination of events, Moss was not selected in the draft until the Minnesota Vikings took him with the twenty-first pick. He promised to use this snub as an incentive to do even better when playing the teams that passed him over.

An Impressive Rookie Season

When he joined the team, Moss was taken under the wing of veteran Minnesota receiver Cris Carter. The rookie began working out with the veteran, impressing him with his talents. The results of their work were immediately evident. Moss caught fourteen passes for 223 yards and four touchdowns as the Vikings won all four of their preseason games.

Moss did not miss a beat when the regular season started. In Minnesota's very first game, he scored a pair of touchdowns to help lead the Vikings to a 31–7 thrashing of the Tampa Bay Buccaneers. On his very first score, he gave an indication of the kind of athletic play he was capable of making. On a long pass from quarterback Brad Johnson, Moss had to turn back for the ball, which had been underthrown. Using his height and leaping ability, he tapped it away from the defensive back who was hoping for an interception and caught it himself for the touchdown.

Over the ensuing weeks, Moss combined for several long scores with Randall Cunningham, who had replaced Johnson when he broke his leg in the second week of the season. The two combined on numerous "fade passes" for long gains. On this play, Moss would head down the sideline and Cunningham would throw the ball high and to the outside. Moss's leaping ability would usually allow him to reach the ball. If he couldn't, it would go out of bounds with no chance of being intercepted.

Moss had many big games over the course of the season. He caught five passes for 190 yards and two touchdowns against the defending NFC-champion Green Bay Packers in a 37–24 Minnesota win. He scored on three long touchdowns (51, 56, and 56 yards) in a game against the Dallas Cowboys, and three more against the Chicago Bears. All told, Moss posted a rookie record seventeen touchdown receptions as Minnesota went 15–1 during the regular season. The Vikings scored a single-season record 556 points for the year.

Moss added two more scores in the play-offs, but the Vikings fell to the Atlanta Falcons in the NFC championship contest to

Moss hurdles a New England Patriots defender.

come up short in their drive to the Super Bowl. Moss capped his freshman season by being named the NFC Rookie of the Year. He also earned his first Pro Bowl selection. Moss impressed everyone who saw him play, particularly teammate Carter. "My brother [Butch] played pro basketball," said the veteran, "so I was around when guys like Magic [Johnson] and [Larry] Bird were coming in. Do you understand that this kid could be Michael Jordan? That we're on the ground floor of something huge?"[89]

All-Pro Years

Moss followed up his rookie season with another pair of All-Pro years. In 1999, he set a team record for receiving yards with 1,413. In compiling that total, he set a Minnesota mark for 100-yard receiving games in a season with seven. He caught a total of eighty passes, including a 67-yard reception for a touchdown against Detroit in the final game of the year. Against the Bears, he captured a career-high twelve passes for 204 yards (another career high). Moss's touchdown total dropped off to eleven (including one scored on a 64-yard punt return against the Kansas City Chiefs), but he still was selected to the Pro Bowl for the second time. There, he caught nine passes for 212 yards and one touchdown to lead the NFC to a 51–31 victory over the AFC. For his effort, Moss was named the game's Most Valuable Player.

In 2000, Moss earned his third straight trip to the Pro Bowl. He broke his own Vikings single-season record for receiving yards by accumulating 1,437 on seventy-seven receptions. His fifteen touchdown catches led the league for the second time in his three seasons. He set another team mark by gaining more than 100 yards receiving on eight occasions. On December 17, he connected with quarterback Daunte Culpepper on a 78-yard touchdown for the longest scoring catch of his pro career.

Despite Moss's heroics, the Vikings came up short of the Super Bowl in both seasons. In 1999, they defeated the Cowboys, 27–10, in the NFC wild card game before losing to the eventual Super Bowl champion St. Louis Rams, 49–37, in the NFC divisional play-off. The following year, Minnesota bested the Saints, 34–16, in the divisional play-off. In the NFC championship game, however, they were embarrassed by the New York Giants, losing by a 41–0 count. It was the second-worst play-off loss in NFL history. Frustrated by the defeat, Moss hinted that he might leave Minnesota in the future. "I'm going to have a Super Bowl ring," he said. "I can't really say I'm going to be a Minnesota Viking in a couple of years."[90]

Moss Versus the NFL

After just three years in the league, Moss had established himself as one of the best players in the NFL. However, there were also some on-field incidents that caught the attention of the league office. The first of these occurred during the 1999 post-season loss to the Rams. Frustrated by his failure to get a pass interference call on one play, Moss foolishly squirted field judge Jim Saracino with a water bottle. He was fined $40,000 for the episode, but the fine was later reduced to $25,000 on the condition that he remain out of trouble. Moss agreed to pay the remaining $15,000 if he had any further run-ins with officials.

The next November, he was fined $25,000 for making contact with an official during Minnesota's 41–13 loss to the Tampa Bay Buccaneers. Many observers, including Moss's agent Dante DiTrapano, thought the fine was too severe. "Randy is disappointed the league levied such an excessive fine," said Di-Trapano, "considering his conduct in this instance. Touching the field judge's elbow did not fall into the same category as his prior violation, for which he has accepted responsibility and paid large fines."[91]

In addition to his scrapes with the officials, Moss's attitude on the field came under close scrutiny. Although the Vikings won their first four games of the 2000 season, Moss often gave the appearance of being bored or disinterested. He often gave little effort on plays that were not run for him. As one coach said, "Most guys would have been benched or cut. But this guy is such an incredible talent, you can't do that to him."[92]

After a loss to the Rams in December, Moss's play was ana-lyzed by St. Louis cornerback Todd Lyght. "When he isn't the primary receiver," said Lyght, "he'll take a play off. If it's a run away from him, he'll shut it down."[93] Moss did not deny the al-legations. "It doesn't really bother me," he said, "when people talk about me taking plays off. It only bothers me when I'm on the field and I take a play off, and the ball's thrown and I'm not where I should be. . . . Only when something bad happens on the field." [94]

More Mistakes

Despite the controversy concerning Moss's attitude, the Vikings felt they could not afford to let him take his talent to another team. Over the summer of 2001, Moss reached an agreement with Minnesota officials on an extension of his contract that

Moss poses for the camera after signing a contract with sporting goods manufacturer Nike in 1999.

made him the third-highest-paid player in the league. The $75 million, eight-year contract included an $18 million signing bonus. "I've been planning on this day for a long time," he said. "Security for me and my family is now here."[95]

Once play began, however, Moss's problems resumed. Early in the preseason, he was fined $5,000 by the league for wearing a hat that was not produced by the official hat sponsor of the NFL. During the regular season, he was fined three times for taunting.

In late November, Moss told a writer from the *Minneapolis Star Tribune*, "I play when I want to play. Do I play up to my top performance, my ability, every time? Maybe not. . . . Case closed."[96] Talking to a group of Tennessee writers a couple of weeks later, he added, "There is nobody on the face of this earth to make me go out there and play football. When I want to play at my highest level, I'll do that."[97]

Moss's performance in 2001 reflected his attitude. Although he caught a career-high eighty-two passes, his receiving yardage was more than two hundred yards less than in 2000. He caught a career-low ten scoring passes and had just four plays of forty or more yards.

Vikings head coach Dennis Green refused to step up and discipline Moss. By failing to do so, he began to lose control of the team. Minnesota's record fell to 5–11 for the year and Green was fired. He was replaced by former offensive line coach Mike Tice.

Hope for the Future?

Tice did not foresee any difficulties dealing with Moss. "Randy Moss is not a problem," he said. "Randy knows my stance. I'm up front with him and I'll let him know what I think."[98]

He also said, however, that Moss would no longer be able to do whatever he wants whenever he wants to. "I'm not going to treat Randy one way," he said, "and have a separate set of rules for everybody else. Everybody has to adhere to them."[99]

Whether Tice is able to prevent Moss from self-destructing remains to be seen. His plans for using him on the field, however, have been met with eager approval by the enigmatic receiver. After studying each game of the 2001 season in depth, Tice came up with a simple conclusion. "When we throw the ball in Randy's direction," he said, "we win football games."[100]

With this in mind, Tice plans to get Moss at least two receptions per quarter. Such a pace would give him 128 catches for the year, which is 5 more than the current NFL record. Not surprisingly, Moss is all in favor of Tice's game plan. "It's a proven fact," he says, "when I touch the ball we win."[101]

Moss is the only wide receiver in NFL history to record one-thousand-yard seasons in each of his first four years in the league. He has the potential to become the greatest receiver the league has ever seen. If Tice can get him to fulfill that potential, the Vikings may yet reach their dream of a Super Bowl championship.

Coach Mike Tice (right) approaches Moss during the 2001 preseason.

Minnesota Vikings Achievements

Year	W–L–T	PF	PA
2001	5–11–0	290	390
2000	11–5–0	397	371
1999	10–6–0	399	335
1998	15–1–0	556	296
1997	9–7–0	354	359
1996	9–7–0	298	315
1995	8–8–0	412	385
1994	10–6–0	356	314
1993	9–7–0	277	290
1992	11–5–0	374	249
1991	8–8–0	301	306
1990	6–10–0	351	326
1989	10–6–0	351	275
1988	11–5–0	406	233
1987	8–7–0	336	335
1986	9–7–0	398	273
1985	7–9–0	346	359
1984	3–13–0	276	484
1983	8–8–0	316	348
1982	5–4–0	187	198

1981	7–9–0	325	369
1980	9–7–0	317	308
1979	7–9–0	259	337
1978	8–7–1	294	306
1977	9–5–0	231	227
1976	11–2–1	305	176
1975	12–2–0	377	180
1974	10–4–0	310	195
1973	12–2–0	296	168
1972	7–7–0	301	252
1971	11–3–0	245	139
1970	12–2–0	335	143
1969	12–2–0	379	133
1968	8–6–0	282	242
1967	3–8–3	233	294
1966	4–9–1	292	304
1965	7–6–0	362	362
1964	8–5–1	355	296
1963	5–8–1	309	390
1962	2–11–1	254	410
1961	3–11–0	285	407

Passing Leaders
National Football Conference 1970–

Year	Player, Team	Att	Cmp	Yds	TD	Rtg
1975	Fran Tarkenton, Minnesota	425	273	2,994	25	91.7
1986	Tommy Kramer, Minnesota	372	208	3,000	24	92.6
1988	Wade Wilson, Minnesota	332	204	2,746	15	91.5
1998	Randall Cunningham, Minnesota	425	259	3,704	34	106.0

Rushing Leaders
National Football Conference 1970–

Year	Player, Team	Att	Yds	Avg	TD
2000	Robert Smith, Minnesota	295	1,521	5.2	7

Pass Reception Leaders
National Football Conference 1970–

Year	Player, Team	No.	Yds	Avg	TD
1975	Chuck Foreman, Minnesota	73	691	9.5	9
1977	Ahmad Rashad, Minnesota	51	681	13.4	2
1978	Rickey Young, Minnesota	88	704	8.0	5
1979	Ahmad Rashad, Minnesota	80	1,156	14.5	9
1994	Cris Carter, Minnesota	122	1,256	10.3	7

Scoring Leaders
National Football League 1932–69

Year	Player, Team	TD	FG	PAT	Pts
1969	Fred Cox, Minnesota	0	26	43	121

National Football Conference 1970–

Year	Player, Team	TD	FG	PAT	Pts
1970	Fred Cox, Minnesota	0	30	35	125
1975	Chuck Foreman, Minnesota	22	0	0	132
1994	Emmitt Smith, Dallas	22	0	0	132
TIE	Fuad Reveiz, Minnesota	0	34	30	132
1998	Gary Anderson, Minnesota	0	35	59	164

Interception Leaders
National Football Conference 1970–

Year	Player, Team	No.
1973	Bobby Bryant, Minnesota	7
1975	Paul Krause, Minnesota	10
1992	Audray McMillian, Minnesota	8
1995	Orlando Thomas, Minnesota	9

Punting Leaders
National Football League 1939–69

Year	Player, Team	Ave.
1964	Bobby Walden, Minnesota	46.4

National Football Conference 1970–

Year	Player, Team	Ave.
1991	Harry Newsome, Minnesota	45.5
1992	Harry Newsome, Minnesota	45.0
1999	Mitch Berger, Minnesota	45.4
2000	Mitch Berger, Minnesota	44.7

Punt Return Leaders
National Football Conference 1970–

Year	Player, Team	Ave.
1995	David Palmer, Minnesota	13.2
1997	David Palmer, Minnesota	13.1

Kickoff Return Leaders
National Football Conference 1970–

Year	Player, Team	Ave.
1979	Jimmy Edwards, Minnesota	25.1
1983	Darrin Nelson, Minnesota	24.7

NFL's Most Valuable Player/
Player of the Year

Year	Player	Position	Team
1971	Alan Page	DT	Minnesota
	(Associated Press)		
1975	Fran Tarkenton	QB	Minnesota
	(Pro Football Writers of America, Associated Press, Newspaper Enterprise Association, Maxwell Club of Philadelphia)		
1998	Randall Cunningham	QB	Minnesota
	(Maxwell Club of Philadelphia)		

NFC Player of the Year

Year	Player	Position	Team
1971	Alan Page	DT	Minnesota
1975	Fran Tarkenton	QB	Minnesota
1976	Chuck Foreman	RB	Minnesota
1989	Def - Keith Millard	DT	Minnesota
1992	Def - Chris Doleman	DE	Minnesota

NFL's Offensive Player of the Year

Year	Player	Position	Team
1975	Fran Tarkenton	QB	Minnesota

NFL's Defensive Player of the Year

Year	Player	Position	Team
1971	Alan Page	DT	Minnesota
1989	Keith Millard	DT	Minnesota

NFL's Rookie of the Year

Year	Player	Position	Team
1963	Paul Flatley	OE	Minnesota
	(Associated Press, United Press, *The Sporting News*)		
1973	Chuck Foreman	RB	Minnesota
	(*Pro Football Weekly*)		
1998	Randy Moss	WR	Minnesota
	(Pro Football Writers of America, *The Sporting News*)		

NFL/NFC Rookie of the Year

Year	Player	Position	Team
1963	Paul Flatley	FL	Minnesota
1976	Sammy White	WR	Minnesota

NFL Offensive Rookie of the Year

Year	Player	Position	Team
1973	Chuck Foreman	RB	Minnesota
1976	Sammy White	WR	Minnesota
1998	Randy Moss	WR	Minnesota

NFL Coach of the Year

Year	Coach	League	Team
1969	Bud Grant	NFL	Minnesota
1992	Dennis Green	NFC	Minnesota

Notes

Chapter 1: Always a Bridesmaid

1. Quoted in "The Vikings Timeline," *Viking Update*, July 19, 2001. www.vikings.theinsiders.com.
2. Quoted in Tom Bennett, David Boss, Jim Campbell, Seymour Siwoff, Rick Smith, and John Wiebusch, eds., *The NFL's Official Encyclopedic History of Professional Football.* New York: Macmillan Publishing, 1977, p. 164.
3. Quoted in "The Vikings Timeline."
4. Quoted in Anthony Holden, "The Purple People-Eaters," *CBS SportsLine.* www.cbs.sportsline.com.
5. Quoted in "The Famous Hail Mary Pass," *Viking Update*, July 20, 2001. www.vikings.theinsiders.com.
6. Quoted in Bennett et al., eds. *The NFL's Official Encyclopedic History of Professional Football*, p. 165.
7. Quoted in Jim Klobuchar, *Knights and Knaves of Autumn.* Cambridge, MN: Adventure Publications, 2000, p. 158.

Chapter 2: Fran Tarkenton

8. Quoted in Charles Moritz, ed., *Current Biography Yearbook: 1969.* New York: H. W. Wilson, 1969, p. 424.
9. Quoted in Jim Klobuchar and Fran Tarkenton, *Tarkenton.* New York: Harper & Row, 1976, p. 37.
10. Quoted in Klobuchar and Tarkenton, *Tarkenton*, p. 39.
11. Quoted in "Fran Tarkenton: The Scrambler," *Viking Update*, July 19, 2001. www.vikings.theinsiders.com.
12. Quoted in Moritz, *Current Biography Yearbook: 1969*, p. 424.
13. Quoted in Moritz, *Current Biography Yearbook: 1969*, p. 424.
14. Quoted in "Fran Tarkenton: The Scrambler."
15. Quoted in Moritz, *Current Biography Yearbook: 1969*, p. 424.
16. Quoted in Klobuchar and Tarkenton, *Tarkenton*, p. 109.
17. Quoted in Klobuchar and Tarkenton, *Tarkenton*, p. 132.

18. Quoted in "Fran Tarkenton: The Scrambler."
19. Quoted in "Fran Tarkenton: The Scrambler."
20. Quoted in Peter King, *Greatest Quarterbacks.* New York: *Time*, 1999, p. 106.
21. Quoted in King, *Greatest Quarterbacks,* p. 109.

Chapter 3: Jim Marshall
22. Quoted in Bob Sansevere, "Former NFL Iron Man Won't Stay Down," *Saint Paul Pioneer Press,* July 17, 2001.
23. Quoted in Jim Klobuchar with Jeff Siemon's Journal, *Will the Vikings Ever Win the Super Bowl?* New York: Harper & Row, 1977, p. 44.
24. Quoted in Klobuchar with Siemon's Journal, *Will the Vikings Ever Win the Super Bowl?* p. 36.
25. Quoted in Nancy Morgan, "A Play That Will Live in Infamy," *Sports Illustrated,* October 31, 1994.
26. Quoted in Morgan, "A Play That Will Live in Infamy."
27. Quoted in " 'My Life Will Continue,' " *Sports Illustrated/CNN,* August 17, 2000. www.sportsillustrated.cnn.com.
28. Quoted in Holden, "The Purple People-Eaters."
29. Quoted in Anthony Cotton, "A Man for Twenty Seasons," *Sports Illustrated,* December 24–31, 1979.
30. Quoted in Klobuchar, *Knights and Knaves of Autumn,* p. 106.
31. Quoted in Sansevere, "Former NFL Iron Man Won't Stay Down."
32. Quoted in "Vikings Retire Marshall's No. 70," *Sports Illustrated/CNN,* November 28, 1999. www.sportsillustrated.cnn.com.
33. Quoted in "Marshall's Number to Be Retired on Nov. 28," *Vikings Mania.* www.vikingsmania.com.
34. Quoted in "Marshall's Number to Be Retired on Nov. 28."
35. Quoted in "Marshall's Number to Be Retired on Nov. 28."
36. Quoted in Don Banks, " 'A Lot of Love,' " *Sports Illustrated/CNN,* August 16, 2000. www.sportsillustrated.cnn.com.
37. Quoted in Peter King, "Written in Stone," *Sports Illustrated,* November 20, 1995.

Chapter 4: Bud Grant
38. Quoted in Bill McGrane, *Bud: The Other Side of the Glacier.* New York: Harper & Row, 1986, p. 18.

39. Quoted in McGrane, *Bud: The Other Side of the Glacier*, p. 20.
40. Quoted in McGrane, *Bud: The Other Side of the Glacier*, p. 30.
41. Quoted in McGrane, *Bud: The Other Side of the Glacier*, p. 46.
42. Quoted in McGrane, *Bud: The Other Side of the Glacier*, p. 50.
43. Quoted in McGrane, *Bud: The Other Side of the Glacier*, p. 72.
44. Quoted in McGrane, *Bud: The Other Side of the Glacier*, p. 79.
45. Quoted in McGrane, *Bud: The Other Side of the Glacier*, pp. 86–87.
46. Quoted in McGrane, *Bud: The Other Side of the Glacier*, p. 101.
47. Quoted in Gene Brown, ed., *The New York Times Encyclopedia of Sports: Football*. New York: Arno Press, 1979, p. 167.
48. Quoted in Sid Hartman, "Grant Resigns as Vikings Coach," *Star Tribune*, January 28, 1984. www.startribune.com.
49. Quoted in McGrane, *Bud: The Other Side of the Glacier*, p. 91.
50. Quoted in Lee Green, ed., *Sportswit*. New York: Fawcett Crest, 1984, p. 101.

Chapter 5: Alan Page

51. Quoted in Jeremy Schaap, "Now He Tackles Injustice," *Parade Magazine*, September 9, 1990, p. 12.
52. Quoted in Michael Fedo, "Close-Up: Alan Page the Defense Doesn't Rest," *Runner's World*, February 1990.
53. Quoted in Steve Rushin, "Thanks, Your Honor," *Sports Illustrated*, July 31, 2000, p. 136.
54. Quoted in "The Purple People Eaters," *Viking Update*, July 19, 2001. www.vikings.theinsiders.com.
55. Quoted in Paul Levy, "Alan Page Raced to the Top of the NFL Mountain, and Found the Journey Was 'What It Was All About,' " *Sports History*, May 1989, p. 59.
56. Quoted in Levy, "Alan Page Raced to the Top of the NFL Mountain," p. 60.
57. Quoted in Holden, "The Purple People-Eaters."
58. Quoted in Anthony Holden, "Alan Page," *CBS SportsLine*. www.cbs.sportsline.com.
59. Quoted in Holden, "Alan Page."
60. Quoted in E. M. Swift, "A Page Out of NFL History," *Sports Illustrated*, December 28, 1981–January 4, 1982, p. 80.

61. Quoted in Levy, "Alan Page Raced to the Top of the NFL Mountain," p. 60.
62. Quoted in Levy, "Alan Page Raced to the Top of the NFL Mountain," p. 10.
63. Quoted in Fedo, "Close-Up: Alan Page the Defense Doesn't Rest."
64. Quoted in Cooper Rollow, "Hall of Fame Profiles," *Sporting News,* August 8, 1988, p. 37.
65. Quoted in Levy, "Alan Page Raced to the Top of the NFL Mountain," p. 59.
66. Quoted in David L. Porter, ed., *African-American Sports Greats,* Westport, CT: Greenwood Press, 1995, p. 243.
67. Quoted in Porter, ed., *African-American Sports Greats,* p. 242.
68. Quoted in Peter King, *Football: A History of the Professional Game.* New York: Time, 1996, p. 150.
69. Quoted in King, *Football,* p. 150.
70. Quoted in "Alan C. Page," *Keppler Associates Inc. Online.* www.kepplerassociates.com.

Chapter 6: Cris Carter

71. Quoted in Butch Carter and Cris Carter, *Born to Believe.* Upper Tantallon, Nova Scotia, Canada: Full Wits Publishing, 2000, p. 77.
72. Carter and Carter, *Born to Believe,* p. 82.
73. Quoted in Klobuchar, *Knights and Knaves of Autumn,* p. 136.
74. Carter and Carter, *Born to Believe,* p. 41.
75. Quoted in "Carter Retires After Fifteen-Year NFL Career," *ESPN,* May 22, 2002. www.espn.go.com.
76. Quoted in Jeffri Chadiha, "Time Trial," *Sports Illustrated,* July 3, 2000, p. 63.
77. Quoted in Klobuchar, *Knights and Knaves of Autumn,* p. 137.
78. Quoted in "Vikings' Cris Carter Wins Walter Payton Man of Year Award," *Detroit News,* January 29, 2000.
79. Quoted in Kent Youngblood, "Cris Carter Announces Retirement, Move to HBO Sports," *Star Tribune,* May 22, 2002.
80. Quoted in Kent Youngblood, "Cris Carter Announces Retirement, Move to HBO Sports."
81. Quoted in "Carter Retires After Fifteen-Year NFL Career."

82. Quoted in "Carter Retires After Fifteen-Year NFL Career."

Chapter 7: Randy Moss

83. Quoted in Gerald Ensley, "First Turbulence, Then Takeoff," *Sporting News 1996 College Football Yearbook,* p. 39.
84. Quoted in Ensley, "First Turbulence, Then Takeoff," p. 39.
85. Quoted in Ensley, "First Turbulence, Then Takeoff," p. 39.
86. Quoted in S. L. Price, "Cut Off from the Herd," *Sports Illustrated,* August 25, 1997, p. 132.
87. Quoted in Price, "Cut Off from the Herd," p. 138.
88. Quoted in Richard Hoffer, "Catching Up," *Sports Illustrated,* September 7, 1998, p. 68.
89. Quoted in Hoffer, "Catching Up," p. 66.
90. Quoted in "Moss Decides to Stick with Vikings," *ESPN,* July 27, 2001. www.espn.go.com.
91. Quoted in "Moss' Agent Says Appeal Is Coming," *ESPN,* November 2, 2000. www.espn.go.com.
92. Quoted in Chris Mortensen, "Moss Must Consider Walter Payton's Example," *ESPN,* October 4, 2000. www.espn.go.com.
93. Quoted in Tim Keown, "Moss Macho," *ESPN the Magazine,* January 22, 2001.
94. Quoted in Keown, "Moss Macho."
95. Quoted in "Moss Decides to Stick with Vikings."
96. Quoted in Peter King, "Cruise Control," *Sports Illustrated,* December 17, 2001, p. 128.
97. Quoted in King, "Cruise Control," p. 128.
98. Quoted in Michael Marot, "Mike Tice Expects Moss to Meet Same Standards as His Teammates," *Yahoo!,* March 1, 2002. www.ca.sports.yahoo.com.
99. Quoted in Marot, "Mike Tice Expects Moss to Meet Same Standards."
100. Quoted in Kevin Seifert, "Vikings' Goal: Two Catches Per Quarter for Moss," *Star Tribune,* April 26, 2002. www.startribune.com.
101. Quoted in "Vikings Receiver Randy Moss Excited About Plan to Get Him the Ball More," *Yahoo!,* April 26, 2002. www.ca.sports.yahoo.com.

For Further Reading

Books

Phil Barber, *The NFL Experience: Twelve Months with America's Favorite Game.* New York: DK Publishing, 2001. *The NFL Experience* takes you behind the scenes and into the inner sanctum of the pro football season from start to finish.

As told to Bob McCullough, *My Greatest Day in Football.* New York: Thomas Dunne Books, 2001. Some of the greatest pro football players of the last half century talk about their greatest day on the field.

National Football League, *The Official NFL 2002 Record and Fact Book.* New York: Workman Publishing, 2002. The only record book authorized by the NFL, this colume contains, among other things, all-time NFL individual and team records, 2001 team and individual statistics, and game-by-game summaries of the 2001 season.

Steve Sabol, *NFL's Greatest.* New York: DK Publishing, 2002. Members of the Pro Football Hall of Fame Selection Committee choose the greatest players, teams, and games and the twenty-five most important events in the history of the National Football League.

Ron Smith, *The Sporting News Selects Football's 100 Greatest Players.* St. Louis: Sporting News, 1999. This lavishly illustrated volume contains brief biographies of the one hundred greatest football players of all time.

Works Consulted

Books

Tom Bennett, David Boss, Jim Campbell, Seymour Siwoff, Rick Smith, and John Wiebusch, eds. *The NFL's Official Encyclopedic History of Professional Football.* New York: Macmillan Publishing, 1977. This five hundred page work covers every aspect of the National Football League, including its history, statistics, records, greatest players, and greatest games.

Gene Brown, ed., *The New York Times Encyclopedia of Sports: Football.* New York: Arno Press, 1979. This volume in the New York Times Encyclopedia of Sports series features newspaper clippings highlighting key events in the history of football.

Butch Carter and Cris Carter, *Born to Believe.* Upper Tantallon, Nova Scotia, Canada: Full Wits Publishing, 2000. An inspirational flip-format book, written by brothers Butch and Cris Carter, dealing with their quest to find their place in a turbulent world.

Lee Green, ed., *Sportswit.* New York: Fawcett Crest, 1984. A collection of sports quotes on a variety of subjects.

Peter King, *Football: A History of the Professional Game.* New York: Time, 1996. A *Sports Illustrated* series volume that is an authoritative tribute to America's most popular sport.

————, *Greatest Quarterbacks.* New York: Time, 1999. A *Sports Illustrated* series volume rating the greatest quarterbacks of all time.

Jim Klobuchar, *Knights and Knaves of Autumn.* Cambridge, MN: Adventure Publications, 2000. Klobuchar's latest book chronicles some of the changes that have affected pro football in the forty years since the Vikings came into existence.

Jim Klobuchar and Fran Tarkenton, *Tarkenton.* New York: Harper & Row, 1976. The biography of the quarterback who made scrambling an effective offensive weapon.

Jim Klobuchar with Jeff Siemon's Journal, *Will the Vikings Ever Win the Super Bowl?* New York: Harper & Row, 1977. A look at the 1976 NFL season and the Vikings' fourth Super Bowl loss.

Bill McGrane, *Bud: The Other Side of the Glacier.* New York: Harper & Row, 1986. The authorized biography of one of the most successful coaches in the history of the National Football League.

Charles Moritz, ed., *Current Biography Yearbook: 1969.* New York: H. W. Wilson, 1969. A library volume that contains all of the biographies published in *Current Biography* magazine in 1969.

David L. Porter, ed., *African-American Sports Greats*, Westport, CT: Greenwood Press, 1995. A collection of biographies of great African-American sports heroes.

Periodicals

Jeffri Chadiha, "Time Trial," *Sports Illustrated*, July 3, 2000.

Anthony Cotton, "A Man for Twenty Seasons," *Sports Illustrated*, December 24–31, 1979.

Gerald Ensley, "First Turbulence, Then Takeoff," *Sporting News 1996 College Football Yearbook.*

Michael Fedo, "Close-Up: Alan Page the Defense Doesn't Rest," *Runner's World*, February 1990.

Richard Hoffer, "Catching Up," *Sports Illustrated*, September 7, 1998.

Peter King, "Cruise Control," *Sports Illustrated*, December 17, 2001.

———, "Written in Stone," *Sports Illustrated*, November 20, 1995.

Paul Levy, "Alan Page Raced to the Top of the NFL Mountain, and Found the Journey Was 'What It Was All About,' " *Sports History*, May 1989.

Nancy Morgan, "A Play That Will Live in Infamy," *Sports Illustrated*, October 31, 1994.

S. L. Price, "Cut Off from the Herd," *Sports Illustrated*, August 25, 1997.

Cooper Rollow, "Hall of Fame Profiles," *Sporting News*, August 8, 1988.

Steve Rushin, "Thanks, Your Honor," *Sports Illustrated*, July 31, 2000.

Bob Sansevere, "Former NFL Iron Man Won't Stay Down," *Saint Paul Pioneer Press*, July 17, 2001.

Jeremy Schaap, "Now He Tackles Injustice," *Parade Magazine*, September 9, 1990.

E. M. Swift, "A Page Out of NFL History," *Sports Illustrated*, December 28, 1981–January 4, 1982.

"Vikings' Cris Carter Wins Walter Payton Man of Year Award," *Detroit News*, January 29, 2000.

Kent Youngblood, "Cris Carter Announces Retirement, Move to HBO Sports," *Star Tribune*, May 22, 2002.

Internet Sources

"Alan C. Page," *Keppler Associates Inc. Online.* www.keppler associates.com.

Don Banks, " 'A Lot of Love,' " *Sports Illustrated/CNN*, August 16, 2000. www.sportsillustrated.cnn.com.

"Carter Retires After Fifteen-Year NFL Career," *ESPN*, May 22, 2002. www.espn.go.com.

"The Famous Hail Mary Pass," *Viking Update*, July 20, 2001. www.vikings.theinsiders.com.

"Fran Tarkenton: The Scrambler," *Viking Update*, July 19, 2001. www.vikings.theinsiders.com.

Sid Hartman, "Grant Resigns as Vikings Coach," *Star Tribune*, January 28, 1984. www.startribune.com.

Anthony Holden, "Alan Page," *CBS SportsLine.* www.cbs.sports line.com.

———, "The Purple People-Eaters," *CBS SportsLine.* www.cbs.sports line.com.

Tim Keown, "Moss Macho," *ESPN the Magazine*, January 22, 2001.

Michael Marot, "Mike Tice Expects Moss to Meet Same Standards as His Teammates," *Yahoo!*, March 1, 2002. www.ca.sports.yahoo.com.

"Marshall's Number to Be Retired on Nov. 28," *Vikings Mania.* www.vikingsmania.com.

Chris Mortensen, "Moss Must Consider Walter Payton's Example," *ESPN*, October 4, 2000. www.espn.go.com.

"Moss' Agent Says Appeal Is Coming," *ESPN*, November 2, 2000. www.espn.go.com.

"Moss Decides to Stick with Vikings," *ESPN*, July 27, 2001. www.espn.go.com.

"My Life Will Continue," *Sports Illustrated/CNN*, August 17, 2000. www.sportsillustrated.cnn.com.

"The Purple People Eaters," *Viking Update*, July 19, 2001. www.vikings.theinsiders.com.

Kevin Seifert, "Vikings' Goal: Two Catches Per Quarter for Moss," *Star Tribune*, April 26, 2002. www.startribune.com.

"Vikings Receiver Randy Moss Excited About Plan to Get Him the Ball More," *Yahoo!*, April 26, 2002. www.ca.sports.yahoo.com.

"Vikings Retire Marshall's No. 70," *Sports Illustrated/CNN*, November 28, 1999. www.sportsillustrated.cnn.com.

"The Vikings Timeline," *Viking Update*, July 19, 2001. www.vikings.theinsiders.com.

Index

Picture Credits

About the Author

John F. Grabowski is a native of Brooklyn, New York. He holds a bachelor's degree in psychology from City College of New York and a master's degree in educational psychology from Teacher's College, Columbia University. He has been a teacher for thirty-three years, as well as a freelance writer, specializing in the fields of sports, education, and comedy. His body of published work includes forty books; a nationally syndicated sports column; consultation on several math textbooks; articles for newspapers, magazines, and the programs of professional sports teams; and comedy material sold to Jay Leno, Joan Rivers, Yakov Smirnoff, and numerous other comics. He and his wife, Patricia, live in Staten Island with their daughter, Elizabeth.